A Troubled History
The Governance of Higher Education in Mississippi

David G. Sansing

Nautilus Publishing Company

A Troubled History, The Governance of Higher Education in Mississipppi
© copyright, 2015, David G. Sansing. All rights reserved. No part of this book may be reproduced without the express, written consent of the publisher except in the case of brief quotations embodied in critical articles and reviews.

For information contact
Nautilus Publishing, 426 South Lamar Blvd., Suite 16, Oxford, MS 38655.

ISBN: 978-193694658-7

The Nautilus Publishing Company
426 South Lamar Blvd., Suite 16, Oxford, Mississippi 38655
Tel: 662-513-0159
www.nautiluspublishing.com

First Edition

Front cover photo by ThinkStock.

Library of Congress Cataloging-in-Publication Data has been applied for.

10   9   8   7   6   5   4   3   2   1

To
Students, Faculty, Staff,
Members of the Boards of Trustees,
Members of the Legislature,
And
The People of Mississippi Who Pay For It All

A Troubled History
The Governance of Higher Education in Mississippi

Introduction		7
Chapter 1	Old Time Colleges in Mississippi, 1798-1840	9
Chapter 2	Founding the State University, 1840-1865	21
Chapter 3	Governing Rival Institutions, 1865-1900	33
Chapter 4	Governing a System of Higher Education, 1900-1928	49
Chapter 5	The Bilbo Purge, 1928-1932	61
Chapter 6	A Constitutional Board of Trustees, 1932-1945	77
Chapter 7	Governing the College Boom, 1945-1962	91
Chapter 8	The Meredith Crisis, 1962-1963	103
Chapter 9	Higher Education in Troubled Times, 1963-1972	115
Chapter 10	Governing a System of Universities, 1972-2000	127
Chapter 11	Restructuring the Governance of Higher Education, 2000-2015	141
Index		155

Introduction

Colleges and universities are dynamic institutions that are in a state of constant motion and change. The modern American university bears little resemblance to its historical forebear, Harvard College, founded in 1636. Before the Civil War most colleges, or seminaries of learning as they were sometimes called, provided religious instruction and a classical education to America's elite minority, and in the South to the sons and daughters of the gentry. The Civil War, and the industrial revolution that followed, secularized American institutions of higher learning and broadened the college curriculum.

In the early twentieth century the nature and function of American colleges were fundamentally altered as the alumni movement and intercollegiate athletics appeared with enormous impact. "The alumni movement," wrote Frederick Rudolph, "had its own rationale, its own purposes, its own life, and [was remote] from the purposes of the professors." Robert Maynard Hutchins described college as "one of life's climactic experiences [that] grows rosier in memory as it recedes in time [and] renewed contact with intercollegiate athletics revives [our] youth as no other experience could." The American college campus became a self contained community with its own traditions and value system, and student publications became a major influence in creating college traditions.

After World War II, the GI Bill and the college boom democratized American institutions of higher learning, and the 1954 Brown Decision eventually opened the college gates to all Americans.

As America entered the twenty-first century, many colleges had become large comprehensive universities and had assumed the nature of "a corporate enterprise...congruent in all major respects with free-enterprise-capitalism [and] adept in marketing themselves."

Through the long and troubled history of higher education in Mississippi, legislators who fund them, and trustees who govern them, have found colleges and universities to be "organized anarchies" that are difficult to govern. As institutions of higher learning change, so must the system of governance keep pace and also change.

This volume is a condensed, revised, and updated version of my earlier study, *Making Haste Slowly: The Troubled History of Higher Education in Mississippi*, that was published in 1990 by the University Press of Mississippi. My original intent was to write a biography of Dr. Verner Smith Holmes, a distinguished member of the Board of Trustees who served two twelve-year terms. Verner Holmes was an Ole Miss alumnus, a classmate and lifetime friend of Governor James P. Coleman who appointed him to the College Board in 1956, and a graduate of The University of Mississippi Medical Center. Dr. Holmes was a remarkable man and suggested, rather than a biography of him, that I write a history of higher education in Mississippi. I agreed to do so and he made his extensive collection of public records and his personal letters and reminiscences available to me. Those documents are reposited in the Holmes Collection in the J. D. Williams Library at The University of Mississippi. Chancellor Porter L. Fortune also encouraged me to write *Making Haste Slowly* and provided financial assistance to conduct the research and leave time to write the manuscript.

I want to express my appreciation to Leila Salisbury, Director of the University Press of Mississippi, and to Craig Gill, Assistant Director and Editor in Chief, for allowing me to use some of the material from *Making Haste Slowly* in this volume. I also want to thank Neil White, Carroll Chiles Moore, and Molly Beth Shaffer at Nautilus Publishing Company for their diligence in publishing the manuscript in such a tight time frame.

And I especially want to thank Ron Borne, Amy Wells Dolan, Dennis Mitchell, Bill Baker, Chester Morgan, and Roy Hudson for reading the manuscript and making many helpful suggestions. I also want to thank Katie Blount, Executive Director of the Mississippi Department of Archives and History and her fine staff, and Director Emeritus Elbert Hilliard for his years of friendship and assistance during my research at the MDAH.

As always, I am deep in debt to Dean Julia Rholes of the J. D. Williams Library and her marvelous staff, especially Stanley Whitehorn, Operations Manager, Lisa Harrison, in Interlibrary Loan, and Dr. Jennifer Ford, Director of Archives and Special Collections and her staff, Dr. Leigh McWhite, Greg Johnson, Jessica Leming, Susan Ivey, Tara Pawley, and Lauren Rogers.

To Elizabeth, David, Cherish, and Cindy; Beth, Michael, Mary Love, and John; Jeannie, Kimberly, Lizzie, and Perry, I thank you for many things.

Chapter 1
Old Time Colleges in Mississippi, 1798-1840

Our country is to be a land of colleges.
Absalom Peters

Higher education in America had already entered its second stage of development by the time Mississippi was established as a territory in 1798. During the colonial period, the American college in its first stage was the "child of the church" and a "nursery for ministers." At the venerable Harvard, according to its 1646 student code, the "main End of [education is] to know God and Jesus Christ which is Eternal life. John 17:3" In 1754, President Thomas Clap of Yale reaffirmed the notion that "Colleges are Societies...for training up persons for the work of the Ministry." The Enlightenment and the American Revolution changed the nature of higher education in America, and during the ascendancy of democracy and free enterprise, colleges turned from piety to polity and a commitment to the republic became a guiding obligation of American colleges. To the founders of the New Republic "the true use of Education is to qualify Men for the Employments of Life, [to] infuse them with a Public Spirit [and a] Benevolence for Mankind, [and] to make them more extensively serviceable to the Commonwealth." Evangelical denominations resisted the transition of the college from a "child of the church" to the "child of the state" and their clergy sermonized against the secularization of education. In the end, it was the Enlightenment, rather than the Covenant, that shaped the American college.[1]

Preeminent among America's apostles of Enlightenment was Thomas Jefferson, one of the new nation's earliest advocates of public education. In 1776, Jefferson introduced a bill in the Virginia legislature to revoke the private charter of William and Mary College and recharter the institution as a public university to train the sons of Virginia in the art of statecraft. Although that bill did not pass, Jefferson was determined to remodel William and Mary. When he later became a member of its Board of Visitors, he tried unsuccessfully to restructure its curriculum and replace the chair of divinity with a chair of science. Most of Jefferson's early efforts at collegiate reform were unsuccessful, but the innovative curriculum that he later installed at the University of Virginia became a model for other American colleges and influenced academic discussion in the United States for the next fifty years. [2]

Mr. Jefferson's disciple in the Old Southwest was W. C. C. Claiborne, the twenty-six year old governor of the Mississippi Territory. Like President Jefferson who appointed him governor of the territory in 1801, Claiborne believed that education was a function of the state. "The very preservation of Republican Government in its genuine purity and energy," he wrote, "depends upon a diffusion of knowledge among the body of society."[3]

Acting on that belief, Governor Claiborne sent a message to the territorial legislature on May 4, 1802 recommending the establishment of a public school system and a "seminary of learning." The legislature responded quickly, and nine days later sent the governor a bill establishing Jefferson College. Governor Claiborne signed the bill on May 13, 1802. The legislature did not establish a public school system until the 1840s.[4]

Governor Claiborne's recommendation for a collegiate institution made no mention of the need to train ministers or to provide moral instruction. Like many other southerners, especially those from Mr. Jefferson's Virginia, Claiborne's conception of man was influenced more by French liberalism than by New England Puritanism. French liberalism, which rejected the Puritan dogma of human depravity, flourished among southerners in the post-Revolutionary period and more than a few southern men must have given counsel to their sons, in actions if not in words, similar to the advice Mr. Jefferson gave his nephew in 1787: "Question with boldness even the existence of God, because if there be one, he must more approve of the homage of reason, than that of blindfold fear."[5]

The Almighty might have approved of Mr. Jefferson's advice but the Scottish Presbyterians, whom Jefferson called "the most intolerant of all sects," did not. Furthermore, the General Assembly of the Presbyterian Church declared in 1811 that education was "the legitimate business of the church, rather than the state." A resurgence of orthodoxy and intolerance swept the Old Southwest in the opening decades of the nineteenth century, and the evangelical denominations used higher education, even at state supported institutions, as a weapon against rationalism, secularism, and religious liberalism. The shifting emphasis at the University of Georgia is a testament to the success of Southern evangelicals. The university was founded in 1785 for the young men of Georgia, that "they may be molded to the love of virtue and good order." Those republican ideals were predicated on the belief that man was good and noble and capable of ordering his society with just and equitable laws. Later, under its Presbyterian minister-president, Robert H. Finley, the university's primary purpose would be "to militate the condition of man and direct his heart to heaven." The tension between church and state, over who would control the colleges, was a central theme in the early history of the governance of higher education in Mississippi.[6]

The law establishing Jefferson College placed the institution under the governance of a thirty-four member, self perpetuating Board of Trustees. The board was given complete governance over the academic affairs of the college, including admission standards, the curriculum, degree requirements, and student examinations. The Board of Trustees was also empowered to "engage a president and other professors" and to "displace or supersede them at pleasure." Since academic credentials were not standardized in the early nineteenth century, board members routinely examined prospective faculty members in their subject areas. Board members also questioned the faculty about their philosophy, politics, and their religious preferences. But trustees took "effectual care that students of all denominations received fair, just, and impartial treatment during their residence at the college."[7]

After a protracted and often acrimonious debate, the Board of Trustees located Jefferson College at Washington, the territorial capital six miles east of Natchez. With the site of Mississippi's first public institution of higher learning settled, the Board of Trustees directed its attention and a considerable amount of effort toward matters of finance. The board faced the bewildering task of establishing a college without funds because the law establishing Jefferson College had not included an appropriation for either capital construction or operating expenses, and the opening of Jefferson College was delayed.[8]

A promising source of funds became available in 1803 when congress provided Jefferson College a land grant in the unsettled territory along the lower Tombigbee River in what is now the state of Alabama. Income from the sale of that township of land, which is about 23,000 acres, would endow an institution of higher learning and was called the "seminary fund." Generous as the grant was, Jefferson College did not receive any immediate benefit because the township was not surveyed until several years later and even then, so few acres were sold that the proceeds from the land grant fell far short of what college officials had anticipated. Consequently, the opening of Jefferson College was postponed indefinitely and the Board of Trustees did not meet from December 21, 1805 to April 28, 1810.[9]

The Board of Trustees, "humbled by the experiences of the past eight years," opened Jefferson College as a sub-collegiate academy on January 1, 1811. In the absence of state funds, faculty and staff members were paid by the tuition and fees collected from the students. That procedure, however tenuous, enabled the board to open Jefferson College. Because of such limited funding, Jefferson College remained a preparatory academy during its first five years.[10]

In 1816, the legislature provided limited financial support to Jefferson College in the form of a $6,000 loan that enabled the board to open the collegiate department in June 1817. Almost immediately after its opening, the Jefferson College Board of Trustees came under attack from a Natchez convention of evangelical ministers for neglecting the religious instruction of their students. The convention made several other charges against its president, James McAllister, who was "advantageously known in the United States for his profound learning."[11]

President McAllister resigned in June 1821 and Jefferson College was operated as a preparatory academy under several different principals. Destitute of resources, its physical facilities fell into disrepair, and its public esteem declined still further. In its 1825 annual report to the legislature the Jefferson College Board of Trustees expressed its "regrets that the well-intentioned efforts of the trustees have not resulted in [something] more substantial." The report detailed the succession of financial crises and legal disputes which had delayed its initial opening and had forced its suspension on several occasions. The Board of Trustees informed the legislature that Jefferson College was at that time without a principal, without students, and without "any active funds." The suspension of Jefferson College in 1825 left the state without a collegiate institution for boys.[12]

After Jefferson College closed, the only collegiate institution in Mississippi was Elizabeth Female Academy, a private girl's college in Natchez. William Hamilton Nelson cites Elizabeth Female Academy as the first college chartered to grant degrees to women not only in Mississippi or the South, but in the United States.[13]

The dismal tone of the Jefferson College report prompted Representative William Haile of Wilkinson County to introduce a resolution to place Jefferson College under the governance of the state legislature. During the debate over Haile's resolution some legislators questioned the board's handling of college funds, many others expressed a general disappointment that the college had not prospered, and some representatives from the new counties recently established in the 1820 Choctaw land cession recommended the relocation of Jefferson College to a more "central situation."[14]

The legislature revoked Jefferson College's original charter at its January 1826 session and reorganized its Board of Trustees. The governor and lieutenant governor were made *ex officio* members, with the governor serving as president of the board. The law reduced the number of trustees from thirty-four to twenty-four and gave the legislature the authority to appoint board members. Supporters of the 1826 law expanding the state's role in the governance of Jefferson College believed they were securing its future as the primary institution of higher learning in Mississippi. They would soon be disappointed.[15]

In 1829, just three years after the reorganization of Jefferson College, Governor Gerard C. Brandon lectured the legislature on the relationship between "ignorance and despotism." A well-educated citizenry, he said, could not be deceived by "fraud or stratagem." Mississippi was not providing its young men and women the kind of education that he considered essential to self-government. After a review of what he called the "troubled history" of Jefferson College, Governor Brandon recommended its closure and the designation of Mississippi Academy in Clinton as the state university. Mississippi Academy, which had been chartered as Hampstead Academy in 1825, was a thriving collegiate institution with an enrollment of nearly one hundred and, like Jefferson College, it was technically a state-supported institution. The 1827 legislation granting it a collegiate charter also allocated part of the proceeds from a second federal land grant, which Mississippi had received in 1819, to the Academy for a period of five years. The enormous potential of that revenue encouraged the patrons of Mississippi Academy to seek its designation as the state university. But Governor Brandon could not persuade the legislature to create one state institution of higher learning at a central location.[16]

In the early years of the republic, academicians, like entrepreneurs, were infected with the American ethic of growth and greatness. Frederick Rudolph has compared college-founding to "canal building, cotton ginning, [and] gold mining." America's restless money-making people favored a collegiate network that was as dynamic and decentralized as the far-flung country itself. The idea of a national university was just that, an idea, with little popular appeal. The effort to establish a central university under federal patronage where "the youth of all the states" would be molded "into one mass of citizens" was doomed from the beginning because America would become a "culture with many capitals" and a country with many colleges.[17]

Only nine colleges existed in America at the time of the Revolution. By the Civil War, there were more than two hundred and forty, almost half of those in the South. Thirty-four had been established in Mississippi, three of which were in Marshall County. One of those Marshall County colleges was the University of Holly Springs. Its first president explained that the university was the product of a "speculative mania" that had induced the people to project "vast calculations upon slender and uncertain data." The University of Holly Springs "wobbled on for three years" and then "went down, unwept and unhonored." The history of the University of Holly Springs was not atypical of antebellum colleges. It has been estimated that perhaps as many as 700 American colleges tried and failed between the end of the Revolution and the beginning of the Civil War.[18]

The predominant institution of higher learning in antebellum America, especially in the South, was the residential liberal arts college that historians have called the Old Time College. The old time residential college was "a large family, sleeping, eating, studying, and worshiping together under one roof." Discipline was as "nearly parental as possible." Consequently, discipline more often than scholarship determined the reputation of an institution and presidents and professors were sometimes hired because of their skill at crowd control. Faculty members were often required to live in the dormitory and police their students. In most Old Time Colleges students took a prescribed course in Latin and Greek, ancient history and literature, logic, philosophy, and rhetoric. The commitment to the classical curriculum was based on the belief that a classical education would produce Christian gentlemen, and that "knowledge of Latin and Greek was the key to understanding [the] grand body of history, science, and philosophy, [that] together with Christianity [is] the substance of western civilization." Although education of slaves and free blacks was prohibited by state law, almost half of the collegiate institutions in antebellum Mississippi were women's colleges. There were no universities in the modern sense and even the state universities were hardly more than liberal arts colleges, though some of them did include a medical school and a law department. Clement Eaton has found in the Old South's support of higher education a "bright contrast" to its neglect of common schools. Frederick Rudolph discerned in that widespread problem an unwritten law: "Where there are no elementary or secondary schools, there you will find a college." He also discovered an addendum to that law: "Offer a young man the principalship of an academy and he will try to make a college of it." Many years later President William D. McCain of the University of Southern Mississippi extended that law and its addendum to its ultimate conclusion: "I took a small college and made it a big university."[19]

The curriculum and pedagogical philosophy in Mississippi's Old Time Colleges was determined by their individual governing boards, most of which were self perpetuating and included a combination of public officials, clergymen, and laymen. The number of trustees and their method of selection was determined by the legislative charter establishing the institution, and in some cases there were specific requirements for board members. At two of the three Masonic colleges, board membership was limited to third degree Masons. For some of the church schools, denominational membership was required and in at least two cases, the Planters College and Madison College, faculty members were *ex officio* members of the board. Semple Broaddus College in De Soto County had one of the largest governing boards in America. The president was one of the sixty-two members of the Board of Trustees. The law creating this institution also provided that a certain number of board members be residents of Tennessee because a Baptist association just across the state line was supporting the institution.[20]

For all the differences among Mississippi's various governing boards, there were three basic characteristics they shared. First, most trustees were laymen and second, there was no limit to their terms because they were self-perpetuating. Thirdly, they held ultimate authority over the institutions they governed. The 1840 catalog of Jefferson College stated that "The authority of the Board of Trustees is supreme." And the charter of Grenada College, like those of most other Mississippi institutions of higher learning, authorized the Board of Trustees to appoint a president and professors and "supersede them at pleasure." Governing boards exercised their authority through the college president, whose role was more of a surrogate than an executive.[21]

A notable exception to that tradition was Centenary College, which was established by the Methodist Church at Brandon Springs in 1839, but was later relocated to Louisiana. At Centenary College, faculty members were given permanent tenure rather than annual contracts, and they could be dismissed only for cause. In addition to providing for faculty tenure, the Centenary College Board of Trustees also introduced a highly innovative experiment in college governance, which included student participation. The historian of Centenary College referred to this experiment as "something new under the sun." It may have been the first of its kind in America. The plan, designed by President David O. Shattuck and approved by a special board committee, divided the government of Centenary College into three departments or branches: (1) the faculty was accorded executive and judicial authority; (2) the legislative authority was shared by a senate, which consisted of the Board of Trustees and the Board of Visitors; and (3) a lower house was composed of twenty-one students who were elected by the student body. The only restrictions on the student house of representatives were that members must be seventeen years old and that only students fifteen years or older could vote for student representatives. The faculty had veto power over the legislative branch, but their veto could be overridden by a simple majority of both houses. Perhaps the most significant feature of that experiment was the provision that a student could be expelled from Centenary College only "upon a fair trial by his peers, a jury of twelve students over sixteen years of age taken among the students by lot." The *Woodville Republican* reported on January 24, 1846, that the experiment was "eminently gratifying" and was a credit to both the college and the students. However, President Augustus Baldwin Longstreet, who succeeded President Shattuck, persuaded the Board of Trustees to abandon the experiment. President Longstreet, who was later president of the University of Mississippi, contended that "if there be anything in which age never confirms the views of youth, it is the direction and government of a school."[22]

Most Old Time Colleges in Mississippi were sponsored by religious denominations, and Oakland College, which was founded at Lorman by Presbyterians, was a premier example of that kind of institution. Its founding president, Reverend Jeremiah Chamberlain, was the preeminent Old Time College president in Mississippi. In an early version of turning the first spade of dirt, Jeremiah Chamberlain's "own sturdy arm felled the first tree" where Oakland College was built in 1830. For twenty-one years, Chamberlain devoted his life to Oakland and developed it into one of the most successful colleges in the Southwest. Oakland was successful in its early years because it was "above the jarrings of party politics, and far removed from the minglings of sectarian interests." Oakland granted the first college degree awarded by a Mississippi institution of higher learning in 1833, and by the mid-1850s Oakland had provided collegiate education to approximately one thousand students and awarded over one hundred degrees. Its two hundred fifty acre campus with nineteen buildings was one of the finest college campuses in the Old South. On the eve of the Civil War, the Oakland College library, combined with the books owned by the school's literary societies, exceeded four thousand volumes.[23]

Perhaps the best testament to Chamberlain's success as a college president was the fact that the institution he founded survived his tragic and violent death, which occurred during the political canvas of 1851. Mississippians were bitterly divided in that gubernatorial campaign between Secessionist John Anthony Quitman and Unionist Henry Stuart Foote. President Chamberlain, who was an ardent Unionist, was accused of expelling a student for making a secessionist speech on the campus. Although he denied the charges, on September 6, 1851, President Chamberlain was attacked by an angry secessionist and fatally stabbed.[24]

The bitter controversy over secession, which claimed the life of its president in 1851, would eventually engulf Oakland and like many other Old Time Colleges, it would become a casualty of the Civil War. In the second year of the war, the college division was closed. After the war, it reopened briefly, but with only a few students and only one professor. In 1871, after Oakland had closed, the state purchased the Oakland campus and established Alcorn University, the first land grant college and one of the earliest state supported institutions of higher learning for blacks in the United States.[25]

As Mississippi was entering the antebellum college boom in 1839, Governor Alexander G. McNutt addressed an open letter to the state's college presidents asking their counsel in the matter of establishing a state university. Some college presidents thought it was an idea whose time had finally come and urged, even pleaded, with the governor to designate their institution as the state university. Most college presidents, however, agreed with President Chamberlain. In his response to the governor's inquiry, Chamberlain asserted that "A state university never has been, or ever will be, in this *free country*, a real blessing to the community at large." A state university would produce an intellectual aristocracy, he said, and that would endanger American democracy. Education must be available to all, and that goal was best served by a decentralized collegiate system that provided moral instruction as well as intellectual training. President Chamberlain then reiterated his denomination's dictum that education was "the legitimate business of the church, rather than the state."[26]

Despite President Chamberlain's objections and Governor McNutt's own misgivings about the establishment of a state university, the legislature appointed a committee in 1840 to select a site for the state university. That action did not actually establish a state university, but it was the first step. Things take time in Mississippi.

Footnotes Chapter 1

1 For Peters' quote, see Frederick Rudolph, *The American College and University, A History* (1962), 47; on the Harvard code, see Richard Hofstadter and Wilson Smith, *American Higher Education: A Documentary History* (1961), I, 8; for President Clap's quote, see John S. Brubacher, *A History of the Problems of Education* (1966), 448; and for the last quote, see David W. Robson, *Educating Republicans, The College in the Era of the American Revolution 1750-1800* (1985), 7; see also Bernard J. Kohlbrenner, "Religion and Higher Education: An Historical Perspective," *History of Education Quarterly* I (June, 1961), 45-57 (*HEQ*), and John D. W. Guice, "Log Colleges and Legacies of the Great Awakening," *Southern Quarterly* (January, 1972), 117-137; George P. Schmidt, *The Liberal Arts College, A Chapter in American Cultural History* (1957), 23; Donald Tewksbury, *The Founding of American Colleges and Universities Before the Civil War* (1932), 55; for a recent masterful study of higher education, see Derek Bok, *Higher Education in America* (2013); for the definitive and most recent scholarly history of Mississippi that provides context for a history of higher education, see Dennis Mitchell, *A New History of Mississippi* (2014).

2 Alma Pauline Foerster, "The State University in the Old South," (Ph. D diss., Duke University, 1939), 14; Rudolph, *American College*, 36, 40-41; Albea Godbold, *The Church College in the Old South* (1944), 147; for the definitive study of higher education before World War II, see Roger L. Geiger, *The History of American Higher Education, Learning and Culture From the Founding to World War II* (2015).

3 During the early 1800s, the area from Georgia to the Mississippi River was known as the Old Southwest; for a brief discussion of Claiborne's educational philosophy see Joseph Hatfield, *William Claiborne, Jeffersonian Centurion in the American Southwest* (1976), 77-80; Dunbar Rowland [ed.], *Official Letter Books of W.C.C. Claiborne, 1801-1816*, 6 vols, (1917), VI, 100-101.

4 Douglas C. McMertrie [ed.], *The Mississippi Territorial Session Laws of May, 1802* (1938), not paginated; in antebellum America, institutions of higher learning were designated by a variety of names including college, seminary, institute, academy, and university.

5 Foerster, "State University," 2, 4, 6, 212; Clement Eaton, *The Freedom of Thought Struggle in the Old South* (Durham, 1940), see Chapter 3, "Aristocrats With Liberal Views."

6 Foerster, "State University," 216, 234-237; David Robson, "College Founding in the New Republic 1776-1800," *HEQ* 23 (Fall, 1983), 326; for a study of the University of Georgia, see Thomas G. Dyer, *The University of Georgia: A Bicentennial History* (1985).

7 McMertrie, *Session Laws*, [not paginated].

8 William T. Blain, *Education in the Old Southwest: A History of Jefferson College,* (1976), 2-6; J. K. Morrison, "Early History of Jefferson College," *Publications of the Mississippi Historical Society* (1898) II, 181-183 (*PMHS*); William B. Hamilton, "Jefferson College and Education in Mississippi, 1798-1817," *Journal of Mississippi History* vol. 3, 266-7 (*JMH*); see also Sharron Lynn Dobbs, "Jefferson College: A Study of the Origins of Higher Education in Mississippi, 1802-1848," (Ph. D diss., University of Mississippi, 1987); Board of Trustees, *The Charter and Statutes of Jefferson College* (1840).

9 Hamilton, *Jefferson College,* 268-269; for the financial problems of Jefferson College, see Charles Sydnor, *A Gentleman of the Old Natchez District, Benjamin L. C. Wailes* (1938); Wailes was a member of the Board of Trustees.

10 Blain, *Jefferson College,* 23-26; Trustees, *Charters and Statutes,* 16, 76, 77; Sydnor, *Wailes,* 204-205.

11 Trustees, *Charters and Statutes,* 16, 77, 78; Sydnor, *Wailes,* 204; Blain, *Jefferson College,* 84; Morrison, "History of Jefferson College," 186; *Mississippi Republican,* December 1, 1818.

12 Blain, *Jefferson College,* 84; Sydnor, *Wailes,* 205; *Senate Journal 1825,* 12-16, 23, 92, 132, 159, 163.

13 Charles Betts Galloway, "Elizabeth Female College, Mother of Female Colleges," *PMHS* (1898) II, 169-178; William Hamilton Nelson, *A Burning Torch and a Flaming Fire, The Story of Centenary College of Louisiana* (1931), l09; Claribel Drake, "Mississippi's Elizabeth Female Academy, Its Claim to be the Mother of Women's Colleges in America," *Daughters of the American Revolution Magazine* (May, 1962), 96, 487ff, makes a strong case for the Academy as a collegiate institution; see also Trey Berry, "A History of Higher Education for Women in Mississippi," (M.A. thesis, University of Mississippi, 1987); Kathleen George Rice, "A History of Whitworth College for Women," (Ph. D diss., University of Mississippi, 1985).

14 *House Journal 1825,* 23, 92.

15 Trustees, *Charter and Statutes,* 18, 79.

16 Trustees, *Charter and Statutes,* 83-84; *House Journal 1829,* 10, 14-15; Morrison, "History of Jefferson College," 187; *Mississippi Laws 1826,* 23-24; [cited hereafter as *Laws* and date]; Richard A. McLemore and Nannie Pitts McLemore, *The History of Mississippi College* (1979), 7-8; William H. Weathersby, *A History of Educational Legislation in Mississippi,* 1798-1860 (1921), 86; for a recent history of Mississippi College, see Charles E. Martin, *Mississippi College With Pride, A History of Mississippi College, 1826-2004* (2007).

17 Rudolph, *American College,* 48; Tewksbury, *Founding American Colleges* 3; David Robson, *Educating Republicans, The College in the Era of the American Revolution 1750-1800* (1985), 228-236; Daniel Boorstin, *The Americans: The National Experience* (1965), see Chapter 20 "Culture with many Capitals: The Booster College," 152-161; on the continuing effort to establish a national university, see David Madsen, *The National University, Enduring Dream of the United States of America* (1966); while Americans rejected the idea of a national university, many Southern sectionalists advocated a regional university to promote Southern views on states' rights and slavery and to educate the Southern elite. The establishment of the University of the South at Sewanee was partly in response to that sentiment; see J. M. Richardson, "Central Southern University: Political and Educational Necessity for Its Establishment," *De Bow's Review* XXIII (1857), 490-503 and "University of the South," ibid, XXVI (1859), 330-335; John S. Ezell, "A Southern Education for Southrons," *Journal of Southern History* vol. 17, 303-328 (*JSH*).

18 The number of antebellum colleges in Mississippi is based on a compilation of those institutions which, in my judgment, were of collegiate rank and includes all schools that were chartered even if they did not open; I relied to a large extent on Weathersby, *Educational Legislation in Mississippi,* although he did not list the Elizabeth Female Academy as a collegiate institution; see also Charles Sydnor, *The Development of Southern Sectionalism, 1819-1848* (1949), 303-304; Thomas O. Summers [ed.], *Autobiography of the Rev. Joseph Travis, A.M.* (1856), 68; William B. Hamilton, "Holly Springs, Mississippi to 1878" (M.A. thesis, University of Mississippi, 1931), 120, 122; Rudolph, *American College,* 47; Tewksbury, *Founding American Colleges,* 28; the number of antebellum colleges that were established and subsequently failed has been revised downward by Natalie A. Naylor, "The Ante-bellum College Movement: A Reappraisal of Tewksbury's *The Founding of American Colleges and*

Chapter 1 — Old Time Colleges in Mississippi, 1798-1840

Universities," HEQ 13 (Fall, 1973), 261-275 and by Colin B. Burke, *American Collegiate Populations: A Test of the Traditional View* (1987); Burke notes that Tewksbury's figures include all the institutions that were chartered, including those that never opened. There were some institutions chartered in Mississippi that did not open, but there were several more antebellum colleges in Mississippi than the seven that Burke lists on page 308.

19 George P. Schmidt, *The Liberal Arts College, A Chapter in American Cultural History* (1957), 103; Clement Eaton, *The Freedom of Thought Struggle in the Old South* (1940), 216; Rudolph, *American College*, 48; the traditional view of antebellum liberal arts colleges, which depicted them as sectarian, inefficient, and inflexible institutions that reflected the pre-modern attitude and values of their sponsors, and in particular Richard Hofstadter's assertion that they were "The Great Retrogression" in American higher education, has been challenged by a host of revisionist historians; for the traditional view, see Richard Hofstadter and Walter P. Metzger, *The Development of Academic Freedom in the United States* (1955), Part One: "The Age of the College;" for a brief statement of the traditional view and a convincing challenge of that interpretation, see Burke's introduction to *Collegiate Populations*; interview with President Emeritus William D. McCain, Hattiesburg, Mississippi, on January 30, 1979.

20 See Weathersby, *Educational Legislation*, 154-161 for abstracts of these college charters.

21 *Charter and Statutes of Jefferson College*, 1840, 31; Weathersby, *Educational Legislation*, 156; for a study of academic government that is generally favorable to an authoritarian Board of Trustees see W. H. Cowley, *Presidents, Professors, and Trustees* (1980).

22 Ray Holder, "Centenary: Roots of a Pioneer College (1838-1844)," *JMH* vol. 42, 77-99; Ray Holder, *William Winans, Methodist Leader in Antebellum Mississippi* (1977), 138-139, 140, 146, 177, 181;Nelson, *Centenary College*, 128-132; John D. Wade, *Augustus Baldwin Longstreet, A Study in the Development of Culture in the South* (1924), 294.

23 Melvin K. Bruss, "History of Oakland College (Mississippi), 1830-1871," (M.A. thesis, LSU, 1965); Tommy W. Rogers, "Oakland College, 1830-1871," *JMH* vol. 24, 143-161.

24 For a brief discussion of the bowie knife stabbing of President Chamberlain, see Bruss, "Oakland College," 63-65.

25 Merleson Guy Dunham, *The Centennial History of Alcorn Agricultural and Mechanical College* (1971), xii; on early black colleges, see Rufus B. Atwood, "The Origin and Development of the Negro Public College, With Special Reference to the Land-Grant College," *Journal of Negro Education* XXXI (Summer, 1962), 240-250 (*JNE*); for a more recent history of Alcorn University, see Josephine McCann Posey, *Against Great Odds: The History of Alcorn State University* (1994).

26 Chamberlain's letter to Governor McNutt is published in *House Journal 1840*, 310; see also Edward Mayes, *History of Education in Mississippi* (1899), 112.

Chapter 2
Founding the State University, 1840-1865

*The day that witnesses the completion of this magnificent temple
of learning will be regarded as the
dawn of a new era in the history of letters.*

Governor Albert G. Brown.

During the early years of the antebellum college boom, the rivalry between sections and factions prolonged the establishment of a state university in Mississippi. Evangelical clergymen, who regarded "the encroachment of scientific discoveries upon sacred mysteries with profound intolerance," had also kept up their opposition to secular education. Another factor delaying the establishment of a state university was the bickering between supporters of public schools and supporters of higher education. A correspondent for the *Southern Reformer* accused Mississippi's aristocracy of trying to conceal its opposition to common schools while promoting the interests of higher education. "A strict analysis of their conduct," this unnamed correspondent claimed, would expose "a desire to build up and endow splendid colleges [for] the benefit of the rich and privileged class, rather than the endowment of schools for the whole community." Alma Pauline Foerster has found that the Southern gentry nurtured the notion that free schools were "a bounty to the indigent." To Southern aristocrats, education was a luxury not a right, and like other luxuries, education should be enjoyed by those who could pay for it.[1]

All of the objections to a state university, and the obstructions that had delayed its establishment for so long, were finally overcome by a combination of two circumstances. First, the gradual depletion of the seminary fund convinced Mississippi's leadership that the only way to prevent the fund from being lost entirely was to establish a state university and allocate whatever remained of the fund to that institution. Through mismanagement and malfeasance, and because of bank failures during the Panic of 1837, the income from the federal land grant fund had gradually declined from nearly $300,000 in 1833 to only $90,000 in 1845. Every governor from 1819, when Mississippi received its second land grant, to the time of the establishment of a state university, had urged the legislature to establish a public university and to safeguard the seminary fund.[2]

The deepening sense of urgency about educating their sons at home persuaded

A Troubled History — The Governance of Higher Education in Mississippi

Mississippi's leadership to establish a state university. "Send your sons to other states," warned a Mississippi college official, and "you estrange them from their native land [and] our institutions are endangered." His warning was an old one that had deep roots in western history and was perhaps first given by Henry II, who "forbade Englishmen from studying in France." The German principalities established universities "to retain the training [of] secular officials" in their own hands and "to keep the money in the country." Colonial fathers complained that their sons who went off to college at Cambridge and Oxford came back as English men, and they began educating their sons at home. By the early 1830s, as the sectional crisis deepened and the agitation for abolition intensified, the Mississippi mind turned back upon itself. Mississippi took on a siege mentality; it became a Closed Society, and every governor from 1830 on cited the urgency of educating Mississippi's sons at home. Governor Albert G. Brown, who signed the law chartering the University of Mississippi, had long favored the founding of a state university, but for reasons that went beyond academics, and he spoke most plainly: "Those opposed to us in principle cannot be entrusted with the education of our sons and daughters." Governor Brown and the founders of the state university realized that education was the "process by which a culture transmits itself across the generations" and they would indoctrinate Mississippi's youth as well as educate them. They presumed a society's right, indeed its obligation, to defend itself against change and they would use the society's educational institutions as one of the instruments of its survival.[3]

In 1840, having at last accepted the propriety of establishing a public university, the Mississippi legislature appointed a committee to recommend a suitable location. After a prolonged and acrimonious debate, and by only one vote, the legislature selected Oxford, a tiny rural hamlet in the northeastern part of the state. Oxford was chosen over Mississippi City, a town midway between Biloxi and Gulfport on Mississippi's seacoast. The location of the state university in "a sylvan exile" was a conscious choice and in keeping with an entrenched tradition in the short history of higher education in the United States. The unhappy history of town and gown, which characterized the medieval university, created an enduring antipathy between colleges and cities. The statute establishing the University of North Carolina, for example, prohibited its location within five miles of any seat of government or in any town where courts of law or equity met. The University of Georgia was established "as deep in the woods and as far from civilization as possible." The iconic president of Williams College, Mark Hopkins, favored a country setting because "fine scenery" helped build good character. That theory prevailed as long as America was rural and green. But after America was urbanized, educators adopted a more pragmatic approach. University of Mississippi Chancellor Frederick A. P. Barnard, for example, after he became president of Columbia University in New York City, scorned the notion that learning could not flourish in an urban environment. That sentiment, he said, would only have merit "if study were a pursuit to be prosecuted in the open streets."[4]

In 1846, after Oxford had been selected but before the university had opened, the controversy over its location resurfaced in the state legislature. Some lawmakers from south Mississippi spoke boldly of secession and their sentiments were seconded by several south Mississippi newspapers that bitterly criticized the location of the state university. Both the *Woodville Republican* and the *Natchez Courier* wondered if Louisiana would have south Mississippi if it could divest itself from the rest of the state.[5]

Horatio Fleming Simrall of Wilkinson County, the southwestern-most county in the state, compared the location of the University of Mississippi to the "coruscations of the north pole." The aurora borealis "are the most brilliant known," he admitted, "but are not seen or enjoyed by near one-fourth of the globe." So will it be with the state university, "this great 'northern light' of Mississippi. The greater portion of the state," he predicted, "will never derive any benefit from it." Because Oxford was virtually inaccessible to large portions of the state in the 1840s, Simrall proposed an alternative. He recommended that the state be divided into four collegiate districts. In each district a college or university would be established and they would receive an equal portion of the seminary funds. Simrall argued that his plan would permit an equitable distribution of the land grant funds and would benefit the entire state rather than just one section. After a long and lively debate, Simrall's proposal was defeated by a vote of thirty-nine to thirty-six with most legislators voting along sectional lines. Simrall's proposal was the last effective challenge to the location of the University of Mississippi until the 1930s, when Governor Theodore G. Bilbo would recommend its relocation to Jackson.[6]

The law that chartered the University in 1844 established a thirteen-member Board of Trustees who were appointed by the governor. Although the law did not require a geographic distribution of board membership, Governor Brown took special care to see that all sections of the state were represented on the original board. All board members were men. Once in place, the board became self perpetuating and was virtually free from external pressure. The Board of Trustees was given absolute authority over the University. It had the power to appoint the president and faculty and remove them at pleasure, to design the University curriculum, to establish rules of student conduct, to plan and layout the campus, and to superintend the construction of University buildings. The board was also given custody of the seminary fund. But before the board could make any use of those funds, the legislature repealed that provision on the grounds that the land grant had been given in trust to the legislature of the state. The board had the power to govern a university, but it did not have the funds to finance it. Consequently, the board and the University became supplicants before the legislature at each successive biennium.[7]

After the legislature revoked the board's control over the seminary fund Governor Brown sent a special message to the legislature requesting a large appropriation for the construction of buildings at the University. Along with his request for funds, Governor Brown also recommended the establishment of ten preparatory schools at various locations throughout the state. He suggested that $800 be appropriated annually to each of the ten academies, and that they be placed under the governance of the Board of Trustees of the University. Governor Brown said, "Nothing is clearer to my mind than that the college will not succeed without the aid of auxiliary schools." The governor had attended both Jefferson College and Mississippi College and knew of the inadequacy of Mississippi's secondary school system. Nevertheless, his recommendation for the establishment of preparatory schools was not enacted.[8]

On February 25, 1848, the Board of Trustees of the state university adopted an organizational structure and a curriculum that was designed primarily by Reverend John Newton Waddel, a member of the original Board of Trustees. Reverend Waddel was an old school Presbyterian minister, the son of President Moses Waddel of the University of Georgia, and the nephew of John C. Calhoun. The curriculum that Waddel recommended, and the board adopted, was the prescribed four year classical course and was based on the premise "that the foundation of all learning was Christianity."[9]

Under Waddel's plan, the university faculty included a president and four professors. The president was also professor of mental and moral philosophy, rhetoric, evidences of Christianity, logic, and political economy. The other faculty positions were designated as the chair of ancient and modern languages, chair of mathematics, chair of natural philosophy and astronomy, and the chair of chemistry, geology, and mineralogy.[10]

The course on the evidences of Christianity sparked a heated exchange between Reverend Waddel and board member E. C. Wilkerson, who objected to the introduction of such a course at a public institution. Trustee John J. McCaughan, "a pronounced infidel," also objected to the course on Christianity and the appointment of ministers to the faculty. The course on Christianity was kept as a part of the University's curriculum, but both Waddel and McCaughan later resigned from the Board of Trustees. Waddel resigned to become a member of the faculty, and McCaughan resigned in protest of the course on Christianity and to distance himself from a public university that would style itself "a Christian institution." Even though the course on Christianity remained a part of the curriculum and ministerial students were exempt from tuition, and even though four of its first five presidents were ministers, the University was often ridiculed by Mississippi's evangelical clergy as a "regularly organized infidel institution."[11]

There were nearly two hundred applicants for the faculty positions at the University and seventeen for the presidency. The anti-clerical faction engineered the appointment of George Frederick Holmes, a twenty eight-year old historian from William and Mary as the University's first president. President Holmes' inaugural address was a masterful defense of the classical curriculum and a plea for funds to equip the library and the laboratories. At the time of his inauguration, the University's income had been largely consumed by the construction of campus buildings, including the Lyceum, which Holmes called one of the most elegant structures in the South.[12]

President Holmes announced in his inaugural address that the "inquisitional system" of discipline that prevailed at Old Time Colleges throughout America would not be enforced at the University of Mississippi. He asked the students to "pledge your honor as gentlemen that you will not violate" the rules of the college. But his experience with the honor system, which was a rare innovation in the American collegiate system at that time, was extremely disappointing. The University's first class of eighty students proved to be ungovernable and by the end of the first session, only forty-seven were still in school; five had been expelled, eight were suspended, twelve were allowed to withdraw, and eight had absented themselves from the University, their whereabouts unknown.[13]

The failure of President Holmes' honor system and a breakdown of discipline brought scorn to the University and criticism to the young president. Personal and family problems also complicated matters for President Holmes. In January 1849, Mrs. Holmes returned to Virginia with an ill child. The child grew worse and in March, President Holmes took a six weeks leave and went to Virginia. Holmes also became ill and could not return when his leave expired. He later claimed that he wrote to the Board of Trustees, explained his circumstances, and asked for an extension. The Board of Trustees claimed it never received his letters. On July 10, 1849, rather than communicating with President Holmes and determining the reason for his absence, the Board of Trustees declared the office vacant and the next day elected the Reverend Augustus Baldwin Longstreet president of the University. Although President Holmes sought reinstatement to his office, the board did not grant his request. Holmes was later appointed to the chair of history at the University of Virginia where he enjoyed a long and distinguished career.[14]

When Reverend Longstreet arrived for the opening of the fall term in November 1849, he was a towering presence at the University. He was an attorney of some renown, a Methodist minister of considerable influence in the Southern church, a famous raconteur, and he had already served as president of two Methodist institutions, Emory in Georgia and Centenary in Louisiana. Longstreet was also an extensive landowner and a large slave owner. Soon after President Longstreet came to the University of Mississippi, he and Jacob Thompson, President of the Board of Trustees, both of whom were lawyers, initiated plans to establish a law department. The Board of Trustees had the authority to establish a law department but there were no funds to fill the chair of law or to secure a library. In 1854, Thompson made a personal appeal to the legislature for a special appropriation to establish a school of "Governmental Science and Law." Thompson explained that the University needed a chair of law but "not of law alone." The philosophy of government should be taught along with law, he said, because instruction "in the science of government we think of high importance to the southern youth." Though it was hardly necessary, Thompson reminded the lawmakers that "we live in a confederacy of states" and the "political relations of the states to each other are looked at in somewhat different lights according to the geographic points of view." Couching his call for funds within the framework of states' rights, Thompson correctly presumed that such an appeal would not be denied by a legislature so stirred by the sectional crisis of the 1850s. His request for a special appropriation was granted, and in the fall of 1854, the University admitted its first law class. The law course did not replace the apprenticeship system, and during its early years the law department more often trained politicians than practitioners.[15]

President Longstreet considered his Methodist ministry the primary mission of his life, and he was frequently absent from his duties at the University. When the Board of Trustees adopted a policy on absenteeism and threatened to dock the pay of any professor who was absent from class without a proper excuse, Longstreet was infuriated, saying if he could not "attend the sick" he would resign. He did in fact tender his resignation along with a request that the board rescind that unpopular policy. The board did not accept his resignation nor did it revoke the rule on absenteeism. J. M. Henry, an Oxford resident who knew President Longstreet quite well, wrote to Governor John J. McRae that Longstreet's resignation was all a bluff anyway because "Old Longstreet is making too much money too fast for him to be induced to resign." Longstreet's biographer writes of his propensity for profit while he was living in Oxford, "true to his fixed custom, Longstreet did not let slip any good chances of turning over an honest dollar."[16]

The political composition of antebellum college boards often complicated the governance of Southern state universities. The rivalry between Whigs, who were Unionists, and Democrats, who were Secessionists, had been a dignified contest played out in the quiet confines of the board room until the 1850s. The anxiety that accompanied the impending secession crisis brought that contest, and all others, into the public arena where reason often gave way to rhetoric, and good judgement gave way to quick temper.[17]

President Longstreet and his son-in-law L. Q. C. Lamar were states' rights Democrats who engaged in rhetorical warfare with the Whig Party and its shortlived successor, the American Party, whose members were also called Know Nothings. President Longstreet accused the Know Nothing Party of "whispering the students of my charge into midnight gatherings, and there binding them by oath upon oath to everlasting fidelity to its own creed." In 1854, President Longstreet advised the University's graduating class to scorn and reject the Know Nothings, who then accused Longstreet of indoctrinating the University's students.[18]

The spectacle of the state university president trading epithets with a secret political society was an uncomely sight, even to Democratic Governor John J. McRae. Longstreet's political entanglements, among other things, convinced Governor McRae and other public officials that the state had conceded too much independence to the University's self perpetuating Board of Trustees and had virtually forfeited its role in the governance of the University's affairs. As a remedy, Governor McRae recommended the establishment of a Board of Visitors. Since the University was a state institution, he reasoned, it should be subject to the visitation of the state through its regularly appointed agents. A Board of Visitors, according to Governor McRae, would have a beneficial effect on the management of the University and the Visitors' attendance at public examinations would encourage students to better prepare themselves. Finally, the governor said, the affairs of the University "would be brought into public notice" by the various reports that the Board of Visitors would publish from time to time.[19]

The University's governing board was not required to make any kind of public report or otherwise account for its actions except to the state legislature. As a consequence, news of the University was disseminated by word of mouth, editorial commentary, Sunday morning sermons, campaign speeches, gossip, rumor, and innuendo. Governor McRae was confident that the reports issued by the Board of Visitors would reduce the damage done by rumor and innuendo, some of which he admitted was calculated by its enemies to disparage the University. Governor McRae's proposal for a Board of Visitors, which the legislature rejected, was the first effort in a continuing search for a structure of governance that would protect Mississippi's institutions of higher learning from political intrusion, and would also satisfy the understandable desire of public officials to make those institutions responsive and responsible to the body politic.

Governor McRae's effort to expand the role of the state in the governance of the state university's affairs was followed six months later by President Longstreet's resignation, but there seems to be no connection between the two. It was presumed that Reverend Waddel would succeed President Longstreet. But to Waddel's mortification he was passed over in favor of Frederick Augustus Porter Barnard, a native of Massachusetts and an 1828 graduate of Yale. Barnard was also a Whig and a Unionist, neither of which was mainstream Southern. During the first secession crisis of 1851, when he was a faculty member at the University of Alabama, Barnard delivered an oration on the Fourth of July in support of the Union. In Mississippi that could have been dangerous, but Barnard's tact and good humor mollified the "secesh Democrats" in Alabama. As the sectional crisis deepened, Professor Barnard became an increasingly controversial figure at Tuscaloosa, and in 1854 Barnard resigned to take a faculty position at the University of Mississippi.[20]

After Barnard was elected president of the University of Mississippi in 1856, he devoted himself and his considerable energy to the single purpose of making the University one of the major institutions of higher learning in the country. He was tireless in that effort, comparing himself to "a stick so crooked it could not lie still." Barnard attacked the University's problems with an urgency that sometimes brought criticism from his less energetic colleagues and from some board members who favored progress but not change, and from a large segment of the Mississippi press who just did not like that "Damn Yankee." It was during Barnard's five year tenure that the term president was superseded by the term chancellor.[21]

A primary focus of Chancellor Barnard's administration was the modification of the governance of the University. The existing rules of governance, Barnard complained, were "so framed [as] to commit the regulation of the most minute details of administration including even such matters as the ringing of the college bell and the arrangement of the hours of recitation to the Board of Trustees." He was determined to reduce the board's administrative role in university affairs, and at its July meeting in 1857, he recommended a thorough revision of the rules and regulations governing the University. His recommendation, along with a memorial from the faculty for general improvements at the University, were sent to a board committee for study. Four days later Barnard and the entire faculty were summoned before the board and informed that the governance of the university would not be modified. Barnard confided to his colleague Professor Eugene Hilgard that during those long days "there were three or four star chamber days." Barnard was surprised by the board's reaction and told Hilgard, "Before I was President I was influential [now] they treat me as they did Longstreet [and] if I hear from them at all, it is in the form of some official interrogatory, behind which lurks some contingent censure."[22]

Barnard's disappointment in the way the board had been treating him was somewhat mollified by the fact that the board soon reversed itself and significantly revised the governance of the university. On November 9, the Board of Trustees agreed to practically all of Barnard's recommendations and adopted a new set of regulations. The new rules transferred most of the internal governance of the University to the chancellor and the faculty. There are two accountings for the board's reversal. First, Barnard's power of persuasion may have eventually won over some of the trustees who had originally opposed his reforms. Second, and probably more importantly, the board's new president, Governor John J. McRae, endorsed the rule changes. Governor McRae had been designated president of the Board of Trustees by an 1857 statute that amended the University's charter. The new law, which was the legislature's alternative to Governor McRae's recommendation for a Board of Visitors, authorized the legislature to appoint the members of the Board of Trustees and made the governor *ex officio* president of the board. Barnard soon found a friend and ally in Governor McRae. After the University had closed, and as he was leaving Mississippi in September 1861, Barnard met briefly with Governor McRae at the Oxford depot. Barnard wrote of that meeting, "After expressing his regret at my retirement, he remarked to me, 'I shall always have one source of satisfaction in the recollection that I have voted for every measure which you have ever recommended.'"[23]

On the eve of the Civil War, Chancellor Barnard had recommended a radical reorganization of the state university that would transform that Old Time College into a *Universitas Scientiarum*, a comprehensive university that would include all the branches of science and medicine, agriculture, law, classical studies, civil and political history, and oriental learning. Barnard's sweeping recommendation stirred resentment among the college community, especially at the church schools, and among the state press. The evangelical clergy renewed their charges that the state university was a "citadel of atheism," and the press branded that "Yankee Barnard" as a Unionist and the University as "a hotbed of abolitionism."[24]

It is impossible to say what might have been the fate of Barnard's *Universitas Scientiarum* had the Civil War not intervened. As the impending crisis drew nearer, Mississippi's political leadership became more concerned about a man's political beliefs than about his educational theories, and the chancellor of the state university must meet the acid test of Southern manhood. He must be sound on slavery and states' rights. Because Barnard was northern born, known to be a Unionist, and had "the college catalog printed in the north," Mississippi's radical editors denounced the University as "a nursery of Yankeeism [and] with a holy horror [they] forewarned the Southern parent of the danger of sending his son here."[25]

On January 9, 1861, Mississippi adopted an Ordinance of Secession, which was drafted by L. Q. C. Lamar, a mathematics professor at the University. Soon afterwards the students began withdrawing from the University and "eagerly pressed to be received into the army." Chancellor Barnard and President Jefferson Davis asked the Mississippi governor not to muster the student units into the Confederate military service. Sending our young boys off to war, President Davis said, was like "grinding the seed corn of the republic." The Board of Trustees considered reorganizing the University as a military academy but decided not to, and finally closed the University. In the fall of 1861, after the students had gone off to war, and the campus was deserted, Chancellor Barnard wrote a northern friend, "We are inhabitants of a solitude. Our university has ceased to have visible existence."[26]

Footnotes Chapter 2

1 On geographic sectionalism in antebellum Mississippi, see Samuel T. Lyles, "Conditions Relating to Sectionalism in Mississippi from 1838 to 1852," (M.A. thesis, University of Mississippi, 1932), 1-9; Albea Godbold, *The Church College in the Old South* (1944), 149; Charles Sydnor, *The Development of Southern Sectionalism, 1819-1848*, (1948), 60-63; Charles W. Dabney, *Universal Education in the South*, (1936), 350. The *Southern Reformer* is quoted in Alma Pauline Foerster, "The State University in the Old South," (Ph. D diss., Duke University, 1939), 391; John D. Wade, *Augustus Baldwin Longstreet*, 228; for a recent history of the university, see David G. Sansing, *The University of Mississippi, A Sesquicentennial History* (1999).

2 Nathanial C. Hathorn, "A Financial History of the University of Mississippi From Its Endowment in 1819 to 1900," (M.A. thesis, University of Mississippi, 1938), 2-5, 7, 9, 22-23.

3 Wilbur J. Cash, in *Mind of the South* (1941), 93-94, says that by the 1830s "The South was enroute to the savage ideal: to that ideal where dissent and variety are completely suppressed and men became, in all their attitudes, professions, and actions, virtual replicas of one another;"for the collegiate official's quote, see Board of Trustees, *The Charter and Statutes of Jefferson College* (1840), 10-11; Mississippi *House of Representatives Journal 1840*, 17-18 (cited hereafter as *House* or *Senate Journal* and date); *House Journal 1844*, 207, 285; W. H. Cowley, *Presidents, Professors and Trustees* (1980), 18, 23; Foerster, "State University," 2; for the last quote, see Bernard Bailyn, *Education in the Forming of American Society* (n.d.), 14; for a study of Governor Brown, see James B. Ranck, *Albert Gallatin Brown: Radical Southern Nationalist* (1937); James L. Axtell, "The Death of the Liberal Arts College," *HEQ* 11 (Winter, 1971), 330-353, suggests that historians of education should take "a cue from cultural anthropologists [and] make continuity and conservatism our working assumptions about societies and the educational institutions they create to preserve and transmit their ideals and social character;" for a different view, see Laurence Veysey, "Toward a New Direction in Educational History: Prospect and Retrospect," *HEQ* 9 (Fall, 1969), 343-359.

4 Reverend J. R. Hutchinson, D. D., *Reminiscences, Sketches, and Speeches* (1874), 22-23, said it was customary in antebellum America to locate colleges in a "sylvan exile to curb the normal wildness of youth;" Neal C. Gillespie, "Ole Miss: A New Look At Her First President," *JMH* vol 30, 282-283; James Allen Cabaniss, *The University of Mississippi, Its First Hundred Years* (1949), 6-7; Rudolph, *College and University*, 92-93; Lyles, "Sectionalism," 1-9.

5 *Woodville Republican*, March 14, 1846, quoting the *Natchez Courier*.

6 Mayes, *Education in Mississippi*, 133-134; *Woodville Republican*, January 31, 1846; *House Journal 1846*, 232-234.

7 Cabaniss, *University of Mississippi*, 7-8; *Laws 1844*, 227-228; *Laws 1846*, 248-249; James Alexander Ventress, who introduced the legislation establishing the state university, is considered the "Father of the University of Mississippi;" for his efforts in behalf of the University and for his long tenure on the Board of Trustees see Lynda Lasswell Crist, "'Useful in His Day': James Alexander Ventress (1805-1867)," (Ph. D diss., University of Tennessee, 1980), especially Chapter V, "A Gentleman of Scholarly Attainments," 191-236.

8 *Senate Journal 1846*, 14.

9 John N. Waddel, *Memorials of Academic Life*, (1891), 248; *Historical Catalogue of the University of Mississippi 1849-1909* (1910), 74; Foerster, "State University," 197.

10 Florence E. Campbell, "Journal of the Board of Trustees of the University of Mississippi," (M.A. thesis, University of Mississippi, 1939), July 12, 1848; this is a typed copy of the manuscript minutes of the board and will be cited hereafter as Campbell, *Minutes*, and date; Cabaniss, *University of Mississippi*, 10.

11 Waddel, *Memorials*, 249-250, 252-253, 288; Campbell, *Minutes*, July 12, 1848, 459; Cabaniss, *University of Mississippi*, 165-166, note 49.

12 Gillespie, "First President," 282; Foerster, "State University," 342-343; Waddel, *Memorials*, 254; Cabaniss, *University of Mississippi*, 14-17.

13 Gillespie, "First President," 284-285; Foerster, "State University," 344; Waddel, *Memorials*, 267.

14 Gillespie, "First President," 289-290; Foerster, "State University," 275-276; Sansing, *University of Mississippi*, 46-48, 55-56.

15 Mayes, *History of Education*, 142; Cabaniss, *University of Mississippi*, 31; Waddel, *Memorials*, 483; for a history of the law school, see Michael De L Landon, *The University of Mississippi School of Law, A Sesquicentennial History* (2006).

16 Wade, *Longstreet*, 302, 304.

17 Foerster, "State University," 392, 407.

18 Wade, *Longstreet*, 305-306; Foerster, "State University," 413; Sansing, *University of Mississippi*, 72-73.

19 *House Journal 1856*, 22.

20 Wade, *Longstreet*, 310; Foerster, "State University," 414; see also J. W. Johnson, "Sketches of Judge A. B. Longstreet and Dr. F. A.P. Barnard," *PMHS* vol. 12, 122-148.

21 Johnson, "Longstreet and Barnard," 143; on Barnard's tenure at the University of Mississippi, see Sansing, *University of Mississippi*, Chapter 4, "Universitas Scientiarum," 75-105.

22 Campbell, *Minutes*, July 8-14, 1857; William J. Chute, *Damn Yankee! The First Career of Frederick A. P. Barnard* (1978), 160.

23 Campbell, *Minutes*, November 9, 1857; *Laws 1857*, 109-110, 439-440, 447; Mayes, *History of Education*, 151; Barnard, "Autobiographical Sketch," 121.

24 Frederick A. P. Barnard, *Letter to the Honorable The Board of Trustees of the University of Mississippi* (1858); see also Sansing, *University of Mississippi*, 85-90.

25 Chute, *Damn Yankee*, 167.

26 Cabaniss, *University of Mississippi*, 46-49; For Davis' quote, see Barnard, "Autobiographical Sketch," 115.

Chapter 3
Governing Rival Institutions, 1865-1900

It would be cheaper for Mississippi to send all of its students to Harvard or Yale than to maintain so many colleges.

Frank Burkitt

"In a world remade by the Civil War," Frederick Rudolph writes, a small group of ambitious and enterprising educational reformers "seized the initiative in higher education" in the same way that John D. Rockefeller, Washington Duke, and Andrew Carnegie had in big business. It was a gilded and dynamic age. President James B. Angell of the University of Michigan found the public mind so "plastic" and "impressionable" that almost any energetic academic could influence the development of higher education in postwar America.[1]

"Only in the desolated, abandoned Southland" was there an absence of these dynamics Rudolph adds, and then concludes that "southern colleges, like the South itself, could but hold on, hold on to romantic dreams of the Old South that never was." Joseph Stetar agrees with Rudolph and claims that, "no such development was evident in the nineteenth-century South where colleges struggled to remain alive [and] college leaders clung more to romantic dreams and were unable to share in the bold expansion experienced by other regions."[2]

Rudolph leaps to a conclusion that is incorrect and Stetar overlooks the heroic efforts of Southern educators to reshape higher education in the postwar South, especially in Mississippi.

Mississippi established a public school system and provided college scholarships for students who agreed to teach in that new system in 1870; restructured the state university in 1870; established the first black land grant college in the United States in 1871; founded a state supported coeducational normal school for blacks in 1872; established an agricultural and mechanical college in 1878; made the state university coeducational in 1882; and founded the first state supported woman's college in the United States in 1884.

As for holding on to romantic dreams of the Old South, that would come later.

University of Mississippi

The first graduating class at the University of Mississippi after the war was addressed in 1869 by Joseph W. Taylor as "The Young Men of the New South." He told them that they were living in a time "a blaze in the spirit of industry, enterprise, and freedom" and that their New South would need "extensive learning [in] all the various departments of literature, science, ancient, medieval, and modern." Stetar's assertion that Southern colleges were lacking in "students, buildings, and assets" is also incorrect, at least as far as the University of Mississippi is concerned. The University suffered virtually no damage during the war, and when it reopened, almost two hundred students enrolled.[3]

Three months after the surrender of General Robert E. Lee at Appomattox in April 1865, Governor William L. Sharkey convened the University of Mississippi Board of Trustees at Oxford. The board appointed Chancellor John N. Waddel and three faculty members, and announced the university would reopen in October. Most of the nearly two hundred students who enrolled were Confederate veterans who would not have met the prewar admission standards, but Chancellor Waddel said he would not reject the "worthy young aspirants [and would] take them by the hand and raise them from the lower to the higher…departments of education." Governor Sharkey allocated $6,000 from a special cotton tax to fund the university for the coming session, but that meager amount proved to be insufficient and was supplemented by a $50 tuition fee and a $5,000 lottery.[4]

The Civil War disillusioned white Mississippians and they were psychologically unprepared for defeat and the consequences of emancipation. But after nearly five years of tumult, the people of Mississippi adopted a new constitution and elected a biracial legislature in 1869. James L. Alcorn, a wealthy planter and former slave owner, was elected Mississippi's first Republican governor. Among the first measures passed by the new order was a law establishing a statewide public school system, and the reorganization of the University, which was Mississippi's only state institution of higher learning. Under the new statute the governor, who was made *ex officio* president, appointed twelve board members to six year staggered terms. Governor Alcorn appointed both Democrats and Republicans to the Board of Trustees and enjoined them to "purge its halls [of] political factions…that has haunted them so long."[5]

The Jackson *Clarion*, a bitter and partisan journal, proclaimed that the University "had been ruthlessly seized by the Spoilsmen who have determined to radicalize it." Democratic pundits cited law professor Thomas L. Walton, a Mississippi attorney whose theory on states' rights brought criticism to him and the University. Professor Walton taught the law students that the federal constitution, federal laws,

Chapter 3 — Governing Rival Institutions, 1865-1900

and federal court decisions took precedent over the state constitution, laws, and court proceedings. In speeches and lectures, Walton insisted that Mississippi was bound by the Fourteenth Amendment granting civil rights to former slaves and must abide by federal court orders based on that amendment. The Crystal Springs *Monitor* joined many other Democratic newspapers and urged Mississippians to take their sons out of the University because "their minds were being imbued with the worst principles of scallawag and carpet-bag politics."[6]

The attacks against the University by partisan politicians and newspapers indicated that Governor Alcorn's plea had gone unheeded. Not only that, but most of the criticism was unfounded and fabricated. One indication that the Board of Trustees was not ruled by partisan or political bias is the fact that when Chancellor Waddel resigned in 1874, the Reconstruction board appointed ex-Confederate General Alexander P. Stewart to succeed him. The University of Mississippi actually prospered under the Reconstruction government and during that volatile period, whatever damage it suffered came from those who claimed to be its friends.

While Mississippi was implementing its new political order in 1870, American higher education was also entering a new era. According to Laurence Veysey, 1870 was the *anno domini* of higher education in the United States. Two towering figures were installed about that time, Charles W. Eliot at Harvard in 1869 and Noah Porter at Yale in 1871. Cornell and California at Berkeley had recently opened, Frederick A. P. Barnard had just begun his distinguished career at Columbia, and Johns Hopkins University was on the drawing board.[7]

In the *anno domini* of American higher education, Chancellor John N. Waddel transformed the state university from an Old Time College with a classical curriculum to a comprehensive university. In his inaugural address Chancellor Waddel explained his intention to make the University a "republic of letters." The Board of Trustees was persuaded and authorized Chancellor Waddel to study the organization of America's leading institutions of higher learning. During the summer of 1869, Chancellor Waddel visited Harvard, Yale, Amherst, University of the City of New York, Princeton, Massachusetts Institute of Technology, Brown, Michigan, and Georgia. At the board's fall meeting, Waddel recommended an organizational plan based on the best features of Harvard and Michigan. The board approved Waddel's plan and authorized him to implement as much of it as the University's financial condition would allow.[8]

Under Chancellor Waddel's reorganization, Professor Eugene Hilgard, the renowned "Father of Soil Science," established an agricultural course on October 2, 1872, but no students enrolled. There was strong support for agricultural education among Mississippi's agrarian leadership, but the politicians who represented the state's farming constituency favored a rival institution rather than a unit within the old aristocratic state university. During its brief existence, the University of Mississippi's college of agriculture attracted few students.[9]

Tougaloo University and State Normal School

When the University of Mississippi was reorganized in 1870, there were no state-supported institutions of higher learning for the freedmen. Collegiate education for blacks was provided by Tougaloo University, established six miles north of Jackson in 1869. Tougaloo University was established by the American Missionary Society and the Freedmen's Bureau and was governed in its early years by those organizations. Tougaloo's department of education, which was called a normal school in the nineteenth century, "became a state sponsored normal school on January 3, 1872" and received state subsidies. The state also provided tuition grants to Tougaloo students who agreed to teach in Mississippi's new public school system. In the 1870s, Tougaloo University and State Normal School at Holly Springs were dedicated to the education of young black Mississippians, and often found themselves friendly rivals before the legislature in search of funding.[10]

Shaw University, which was later renamed Rust College, was overrun with students when it opened in 1870. To provide training for teachers in the state's public school system, the legislature agreed to fund Shaw University's normal department. Although its original Board of Trustees, and its seven member Board of Visitors, continued to govern the other divisions of Shaw University, a separate Board of Trustees that included the governor, the state board of education, and seven additional trustees were appointed to govern the normal department.[11]

In 1872, the normal department was separated from Shaw University and chartered as State Normal School, a coeducational teachers college. The legislature appropriated $10,000 for a building and grounds for the state's only institution of higher learning for African Americans. State Normal School prospered from its founding until the late 1880s when the state appropriation was decreased, and a new Board of Trustees, consisting of the State Superintendent of Education and the Marshall County Superintendent of Education, was appointed to govern State Normal School. In spite of its checkered history, in 1896 Governor John M. Stone praised State Normal as one of Mississippi's best investments in education.[12]

Alcorn Agricultural and Mechanical College

In their first flush of freedom, Mississippi's former slaves craved education and they stormed the citadels of learning where the "stores and treasures of knowledge" had been secreted from them during their years in bondage. Their craving to know about "the world remade by the Civil War" made many white Mississippians uneasy, and there "was a strong undercurrent of nervous apprehension lest at any time some aggressive negro student should...demand admission to the University, in which case an explosion was regarded as inevitable."[13]

In a widely published letter in 1870 Chancellor Waddel was asked: "Will the faculty, as now composed, receive or reject an applicant for admission as a student on account of color?" Chancellor Waddel and the faculty responded that they would "instantly resign should the trustees require them to receive negro students." The Jackson *Clarion* wrote, "We warmly endorse their stand." But Governor Alcorn chided the "obsequious faculty" and added that they were at liberty to resign at any time. No black students sought admission to the University of Mississippi until almost a century later.[14]

That deferred commitment to educational equality in Mississippi was made possible by the establishment of Alcorn University, one of the nation's earliest state-supported institutions of higher learning for blacks. Alcorn University was established in May 1871 on the old campus of Oakland College, which the state had purchased. Originally, it was to be named Revels University in honor of Senator Hiram Revels, one of Mississippi's most prominent leaders during Reconstruction and the first black to serve in the United States Senate. Senator Revels deferred, however, suggesting the university be named in honor of Governor Alcorn. Senator Revels was named Alcorn University's first president.[15]

Alcorn University's charter granted the institution three fifths of Mississippi's federal land grant funds; the other two fifths went to the state university. The Land Grant funds were established by the Morrill Land Grant Act of 1862 to provide federal funds to agricultural and mechanical colleges. Alcorn's charter established a ten member Board of Trustees who would serve five year staggered terms, with the governor as *ex officio* president of the board. A three member Executive Committee, elected by the board, was given authority to act on behalf of the Board of Trustees. All ten members of the Alcorn Board of Trustees were African Americans.[16]

During the 1874 state election, President Hiram Revels and some Alcorn faculty and students were accused of publicly supporting former Governor James L. Alcorn in his bitter gubernatorial campaign against Adelbert Ames, a carpetbag Republican. After Governor Ames was elected, a legislative committee investigated the charges, and on its recommendation President Revels and "All officers, teachers and trustees were discharged." Governor Ames was authorized to appoint a new Board of Trustees and was given the authority "to remove any member of the board at discretion."[17]

After the Democratic Party regained control of state government following the so-called "Revolution of 1875," Governor Stone, who was lieutenant governor and succeeded Governor Ames when he resigned, appointed a new Board of Trustees and reinstated President Hiram Revels. In his message to the legislature on January 3, 1877, Governor Stone assured the Democratic controlled legislature that the reinstatement of President Revels and the appointment of a new Board of Trustees had restored public confidence in Alcorn University.[18]

The Mississippi legislature enacted legislation in 1878 "to establish and organize agricultural and mechanical colleges and to regulate the government of the same." Under that legislation Alcorn University was renamed Alcorn Agricultural and Mechanical College and was allocated one-half of the Morrill Land Grant funds. The legislation also provided for the appointment by the governor of a nine member Board of Trustees, with the approval of the senate, to serve six year staggered terms. One trustee would be selected from each congressional district and the remainder from the state at large. The law also stipulated that five trustees be chosen from "practical agriculturalists, or mechanics, or selected from both, as may be deemed advisable." Admission to Alcorn A&M was originally limited to male students, but women were admitted unofficially in 1884 and officially in 1903.[19]

Reneau Female University

In 1856, Sallie Eola Reneau persuaded the legislature to charter a public college for women at Grenada. At the time she made that request, there was no state supported college for women in the United States. This remarkable young woman was eighteen years old, a recent graduate of Holly Springs Female Academy, and a school teacher when she petitioned the legislature. Like the state university for men at Oxford, Reneau's state college for women would be funded by the proceeds from a federal land grant. Before a grant could be secured, however, the nation was embroiled in Civil War and no grant was made. After the establishment of State Normal School and Alcorn University, Mississippi's only constituency that did not enjoy the benefit of a state institution of higher learning were white women. Chancellor John Waddel had considered the possibility of coeducation during his reorganization of the University in 1870, and acknowledged that some of the nation's finest collegiate institutions were coeducational. He opposed coeducation because "the association of the sexes in such close quarters impaired the delicacy which was woman's adornment."[20]

Immune to any romantic notion about the superiority of white males, Sallie Eola Reneau accepted the "world remade by the Civil War," welcomed that bold new order, and persuaded the legislature to establish a state female collegiate institution in conjunction with the state university. On April 5, 1872 the legislature, which for the first time in the state's history included African Americans, established a state supported female college and named the institution in honor of Sallie Reneau.

The Reneau Female University of Mississippi was established at Oxford as a branch of the University of Mississippi to provide college level courses for women with the "same and equal privileges that the males have been and are now being taught." The statute named Sallie Reneau "Principal of Reneau Female University, and Vice-President of the faculty of the University of Mississippi, at Oxford." The Reneau University's nine member Board of Trustees included Nathaniel S. Reneau, Sallie's father.

Again, Sallie Reneau's hopes and dreams were dashed. After the United States Congress declined to make another land grant to Mississippi, the legislature repealed the act establishing Reneau Female University. Sallie Reneau, in an effort to accomplish the goal she had first conceived in 1856 as an eighteen year old teacher, would not give up and enlisted the support of her friends in Panola County, who persuaded the legislature to establish the Reneau Female University at Sardis. But Reneau and her Sardis allies could not persuade the legislature to fund the university. Reneau's crusade for the education and elevation of women was a remarkable story and what she had long envisioned was at last achieved in 1884 with the founding of the Industrial Institute and College at Columbus, now Mississippi University of Women.[21]

Mississippi Agricultural and Mechanical College

The statute that chartered Alcorn A&M in 1878 also established Mississippi Agricultural and Mechanical College and transferred the school of agriculture from the state university at Oxford to the new college at Starkville. Mississippi A&M opened the storehouse of higher learning to the sons of Mississippi's industrial classes and it came to be known fondly as the "People's College." Although the supporters of an agricultural college were happy to see its establishment, many of them were disappointed in its location, though the Raymond *Hinds County Gazette* confessed that its worst fears had been unfounded. Mississippi A&M College would not be located in Alabama or Tennessee, the editor happily reported, but in the extreme northeast section of Mississippi, which was the "stomping grounds" of Governor Stone. *The Gazette* accused Governor Stone of using his political influence to locate Mississippi A&M in his "neck of the woods."[22]

Politics may also have played a role in the selection of its first president, General Stephen D. Lee, a West Point graduate and a former Confederate general. As a member of the state senate in 1878 President Lee had supported the bill establishing the agricultural college. His support for the advancement of agricultural science may have stemmed from his own well-known failure as a farmer after the Civil War. General Lee was selected over two out-of-state applicants.[23]

During the interval between the founding of A&M College in 1878, and its opening in 1880, President Lee and the Board of Trustees built a campus, assembled a faculty, and designed a curriculum. Of the three, designing the curriculum was the most perplexing. Senator Justin Morrill, the father of land grant colleges, had admonished college officials to "lop off a portion" of the "old, useless classics and fill the vacancy--if there is a vacancy--with less antique and more practical" courses. President Lee was willing to do that and he gave botany, chemistry, biology, and other sciences priority in designing the curriculum. He was handicapped by the fact that the legislature had not appropriated sufficient funds to build a demonstration farm or equip the laboratories and workshops. President Lee was also distracted by the academicians on the faculty who lobbied for the inclusion of classical studies and liberal arts in the curriculum. At their insistence, and in "deference to the wishes of a large class of citizens of the state," President Lee and the board included the classics and liberal arts in the curriculum.[24]

President Lee and the supporters of agricultural education were disconcerted by the greater demand for "book learning" than for "book farming." When Mississippi A&M opened, three hundred and fifty-four students matriculated, but few of them were farm boys. Most students in A&M's first class were sons of well to do families from the surrounding counties in northeast Mississippi. They did not go to Mississippi A&M to study the soils or the rhythm of the seasons, but to prepare themselves for the learned professions. President Lee's own son, a graduate of A&M's first class, had taken a collegiate course and then went off to Harvard to study law.

The founders of the agricultural college had not envisioned A&M as a rival institution to the state university. Frank Burkitt, a Grange activist, a populist editor, a member of the state legislature, and a member of A&M's first Board of Trustees was highly critical of its curriculum, its faculty, and of President Lee. He once said that if the people of Mississippi listened to the "Michigan professor who runs the college farm" they would all starve to death. Burkitt's criticism prompted a public debate over the role of the classics in the agricultural college and only two years after it opened, the legislature appointed a special committee to "inquire into the present condition [and] adaptation to the end for which [A&M was] created."

During the investigation that took place on the campus in February 1882, President Lee and several professors and trustees were interrogated by the legislative committee. President Lee explained that Mississippi A&M was "in a period, when if its technical stamp is not put upon it, it will [fail] as most other agricultural colleges have." The existing academic and literary courses were not the problem. What was lacking, he said, was the "equipment and surroundings to make it an industrial college." President Lee pointed out that when agricultural schools were not provided adequate laboratories and equipment, they became liberal arts colleges in fact and agricultural colleges in name only.[25]

Following the committee's investigation, the A&M faculty and course offerings were thoroughly reorganized. By the fall session of 1882, the "traditionalists had been routed from the faculty." More significant, the legislature appropriated $120,000 for buildings, laboratories, and equipment, and to prevent A&M from becoming a local liberal arts college for northeast Mississippi, and a rival of the state university, the legislature established an enrollment quota for each county and prohibited the admission of out of state students.[26]

In spite of everything that the legislature could do or would do to put a "technical stamp" on Mississippi A&M, the nontechnical and liberal arts courses proliferated. As with the transition of the Old Time College to the modern American university, which began with the founding of Harvard in 1636, the transition of Mississippi Agricultural and Mechanical College to a modern comprehensive multipurpose university began in the year of its founding.

Industrial Institute and College for White Girls

In the post Reconstruction era, which was a time of severe retrenchment under Democratic leadership, Mississippi was struggling to meet the needs of its four existing institutions of higher learning: the University of Mississippi; State Normal School; Alcorn A&M; and Mississippi A&M. The state was also subsidizing the normal department at Tougaloo.

Nevertheless, in 1884 the legislature responded to public pressure and established the Industrial Institute and College for White Girls, a multipurpose institution for white females at Columbus. The Industrial Institute's charter established a Board of Trustees with one trustee from each congressional district and two from the state at large. The governor, who was *ex officio* president, appointed the trustees to six year staggered terms. The original Board of Trustees for the woman's college were all men.[27]

The multiple mission of the Industrial Institute and College was to provide industrial and technical education, teacher training, and a collegiate course leading to a bachelor's degree. To prevent it from becoming just another local liberal arts college for northeast Mississippi, the legislature established an enrollment quota for each county in the state. It was generally understood and intended that the Industrial Institute would emphasize technical and vocational training. Its first president, Richard W. Jones, however, announced that the young ladies who attended his Institute would receive "an education as thorough and extensive as that conferred by our best colleges for young men."[28]

While the Institute's curriculum was being designed, the same debate that had taken place four years earlier at Starkville was repeated in nearby Columbus. The collegiate faculty insisted that the girls in the industrial and normal departments be required to take a certain number of academic courses. They found a convincing ally in President Jones, and over the objection of the vocational instructors, literary courses were required of all students enrolled at the Institute. The expansion of the academic curriculum brought sharp criticism to the institution. One of the loudest complaints was that the girls enrolled in the industrial course were not allowed to live in the college dormitory. The Board of Trustees constantly interfered with the management of the school, and President Jones resigned after three years in protest of their interference.

Following a succession of short term presidents and years of internal discord and nepotism, in 1898 a joint legislative committee found the institution in utter disarray. On one occasion President Robert Frazer learned that the Board of Trustees had employed a teacher "through talk on the streets in Columbus." Included in the joint legislative Committee's one hundred and seven pages of testimony, which was published in the *House Journal* in 1898, was a telling statement by President Frazer. Although he did not say it explicitly, he implied that after seven years he was resigning because the Board of Trustees "in the conduct of the affairs of the institution hardly allowed the president that voice which would seem to be commensurate with the measure of responsibility pertaining to his office."[29]

The joint committee, in its report to the legislature, stated unequivocally: "Your committee is impressed with the fact that under present management of the college, sufficient power is not vested in the president by the trustees." After hearing the joint committee's report, the legislature placed several conditions on the 1898-1899 appropriation to the Industrial Institute and College, and directed the Board of Trustees to expand the president's authority over the internal affairs of the institute, especially in the appointment and removal of the faculty and staff. The legislature also directed the Board of Trustees to allow all students at the Institute and College to live in the dormitories. After the resignation of President Frazer, the Board of Trustees made a special appeal to Andrew Kincannon, who was the state superintendent of education, to accept the presidency of the Industrial Institute. In their initial contact with Kincannon, the trustees promised not to interfere with his administration and to seek additional funding for the institution. Kincannon accepted the appointment and the board honored its pledge of non-interference. His administration was highly successful and after a ten-year tenure, he was appointed Chancellor of the University.[30]

Denominational Colleges

During the late nineteenth century, Mississippi's system of higher education included the five state supported institutions, and several denominational colleges. Mississippi College at Clinton was the only antebellum church college that survived the Civil War with a strong financial base and a stable enrollment. Denominational support for higher education remained strong in Mississippi and several new church schools were established after the Civil War. In addition to Rust and Tougaloo, the new generation of church schools included Blue Mountain (Baptist, 1873), Belhaven (Presbyterian, 1883), Millsaps (Methodist, 1890), and Jackson College, which was established in Natchez by the Baptist Home Mission Society in 1877, was moved to Jackson in 1883, and is now Jackson State University.

The University of Mississippi versus Mississippi A&M

Because the state's resources were so limited, and because of the social and class dynamics during the late nineteenth century, an intense and sometimes acrimonious rivalry developed among the state's institutions of higher learning, especially between the state university and the agricultural college. In 1880, the year Mississippi A&M opened, the legislature voted to compensate the University of Mississippi for the loss of the seminary funds. The University's Board of Trustees informed the legislature that the recovery of those lost funds was absolutely necessary if the University of Mississippi was to become "a seat of learning whose renown shall attract crowds from all parts of the earth, as did Cambridge, Bologna, and Oxford of old." It is doubtful that the legislature expected the University of Mississippi to reach such renown, but it did acknowledge the University's right to compensation and thereafter made an annual special appropriation of $32,000, an amount equal to the interest the University would have received had the seminary funds not been lost.

The validity and fairness of that special appropriation was challenged by United States Senator James Z. George, a member of the Mississippi A&M Board of Trustees, who claimed that the original funds had not been designated to a particular "seminary of learning" and that the agricultural college should receive a fair share of the interest on the lost funds. He called the special appropriation "a fraud on the people of the State" and accused the state university of making "forays on the treasury whenever it suits its convenience or its tastes to do so." In a rejoinder,

Chancellor Edward Mayes accused the Senator of viewing the matter with "a jealous eye" and of being "anxious to find fault."[31]

Those ugly exchanges between Senator George and Chancellor Mayes in the press and in pamphlets reveal much about the origins of the rivalry between State and Ole Miss. The dispute was ostensibly about money, but there was more to it than just money. Senator George not only represented Mississippi A&M, he personified the People's College. He was a son of the industrial class and was called "Commoner" by his admirers with the same pride that the Populist followers of William Jennings Bryan hailed him as "The Great Commoner." Without the benefit of a college connection, Senator George was a self-made man in a time and place where lineage was prized above self reliance and he was sometimes taunted for his lack of ancestry.

Chancellor Mayes was a study in contrast. He had a distinguished Virginia ancestry. His father served in two branches of government and held the chair of law at Transylvania University. Mayes began his college education in Virginia and married the daughter of L. Q. C. Lamar, and through him he entered the lineage of the Longstreets. In his dialogue with Senator George, Chancellor Mayes betrayed a contempt for his adversary and a condescension that smacked of class. That contempt was directed not just at George but also at the institution whose interests he defended.[32]

Chancellor Mayes referred to the state university as Mississippi's "most precious possession" and as such, it warranted the special appropriation. If the University was the state's most precious possession, then the Agricultural College was less precious and therefore it must occupy a lower level in Mississippi's educational hierarchy. In the minds of the alumni and friends of Mississippi A&M, that special appropriation to the University of Mississippi in 1880 was incontrovertible evidence that an educational hierarchy did exist, and they were incensed by it. Again, it was more than just the money. It was the insinuation that the University, and the rich kids, the sons of the old aristocracy, still came first. To those aristocrats Mississippi A&M was just a "cow college."

The popular and prevailing notion that the University was the preeminent institution of higher learning, and that other state schools should not look upon it as a rival, was articulated by a legislative committee in 1886:

> Nothing is better calculated to detract from the merits of the [University] than unfriendly remarks....It should not be regarded by other schools or colleges as a rival, but looked up to as affording superior advantages not attainable elsewhere, as pre-eminently superior to all others, and to which all others should be

tributary.³³

The legislature's recognition of the University as the state's preeminent institution, and its call for an end to any more criticism of it, confirmed the claims of the industrial classes that the state university was the last standing bastion of the old aristocracy.

A bitter and often wasteful rivalry between the University of Mississippi and other state institutions of higher learning was paralleled by a similar rivalry between the emerging common school system and the expanding system of higher education. Representative Frank Burkitt, in one of his angry outbursts, accused Mississippi's aristocracy of maintaining several colleges for the favored elite while ignoring the needs of the common people. Burkitt would later claim that Mississippi was spending $150 dollars a year per college student but only $1.50 for students in the common schools, which he called the "poor man's university." The state's educational priorities, he said, should be turned bottom side up. The legislature's response to Burkitt's outburst was the enactment of a comprehensive school law that enlarged and upgraded the common school system and created yet another claimant against the state's resources. As chairman of the house appropriations committee in 1888 Burkitt forced a drastic reduction in the appropriations for higher education. Mississippi A&M's reduction, which Burkitt singled out for special punishment, was almost $15,000.³⁴

Governance of higher education in Mississippi in the late nineteenth century was shaped by the dynamics between a social order in transition and a power structure resistant to change. Because that power structure controlled the purse, the courts, the law, the pulpit, the press, and the classroom, Mississippi was not unlike a totalitarian state. Nevertheless, the status of the common man and blacks and women was forever altered by the Civil War and the Industrial Revolution, and even in Mississippi the Gilded Age was a time of rising expectations. Mississippi's power structure felt threatened by the rippling effect of the widening circle and it was unsure if it could control the consequences of mass education. On the eve of the new century of light and progress and change, Mississippi's leadership "circled the wagons," began to hold on to dreams of an Old South that never was, and tightened its grip on the public institutions of higher learning.

In 1886 President W. B. Higate of the State Normal School was accused by the white power structure of encouraging his black students, by his own example, to be "uppity and ambitious," and he was fired, and the school was eventually closed. President Jones of the woman's college at Columbus had to reassure the Board of Trustees in 1887 that he was not teaching his female students "to demand the rights of men nor to invade the sphere of men [but] those beautiful Christian graces that constitute her the charm of social life, and the queen of the home." In 1888 a verbal attack in the state legislature on Mississippi A&M's "imported scholars," was followed by a reduction of their salaries and an "epidemic of resignations." In 1889, shortly after requiring Chancellor Mayes and his faculty to sign a statement acknowledging that they served at the "wish" of the Board of Trustees and could be dismissed at its "will," the Board of Trustees fired five of the University's eight professors. In 1896 the all-white Alcorn A&M Board of Trustees appointed Edward H. Triplett, a Baptist minister who did not have a college degree, president of Alcorn. President Triplett was not well received by the Alcorn faculty, and the board was so angered by the faculty's reaction to its authority that it dismissed virtually the entire Alcorn faculty.[35]

Each of Mississippi's five public institutions of higher learning was autonomous and each was governed by a separate Board of Trustees. The governor appointed the members of all five boards and as *ex officio* chairman of each board, he was the only link among them. The College Board members were not only political appointees, many of them were politicians and the institutions they governed felt the fury of rival factions. In 1896, the University of Mississippi Board of Trustees included the governor, state superintendent of education, the state treasurer, a member of the state supreme court, two ex-governors, a congressman, one former state senator, and one future United States senator. College presidents were inevitably drawn into political contests, and if they were not on the winning side, they were subject to dismissal. Reprisals often extended even to the faculty.

The mischief of rival factions, and its intrusion into academia, peaked in the early twentieth century. Stirred by the election of Governor James K. Vardaman, the industrial classes and the dirt farmers, who came to be known as "rednecks," were determined to democratize higher education. That determination climaxed in the undignified dismissal of Chancellor Robert Fulton, an episode that eventually led to the consolidation of the individual governing boards. The creation of one Board of Trustees for all of its five institutions of higher learning was the beginning of a new era in the governance of higher education in Mississippi.

Chapter 3 — Governing Rival Institutions, 1865-1900

Footnotes Chapter 3

1 Rudolph, *American College*, 243-245.

2 Ibid, 244; Joseph Stetar, "In Search of Direction: Southern Higher Education After the Civil War," *HEQ* 25 (Fall, 1985), 341.

3 Joseph W. Taylor, *An Address Delivered Before the Phi Sigma and Hermean Societies at the Commencement... on June 25, 1869* (1869), 8-10.

4 On Chancellor Waddel's tenure at the University, see Waddel, *Memorials*; Cabaniss, *University of Mississippi*, 60 ff; Sansing, *University of Mississippi*, 116ff.

5 William C. Harris, *The Day of the Carpetbagger, Republican Reconstruction in Mississippi* (1979), 345-347; for a biography of Governor Alcorn, see Lillian Pereyra, *James L. Alcorn, Persistent Whig* (1966).

6 Harris, *Carpetbagger*, 345-347.

7 Laurence R. Veysey, *The Emergence of the American University* (1965), l.

8 Grover C. Hooker, "The Origin and Development of the University of Mississippi With Special Reference to Its Legislative Control," (Ph. D diss., Stanford University, 1932), 103;Board of Trustees, *Minutes*, June 19, 1869, September 22-23, 1869, August 17, 1870, October 26, 1870; for a brief report on his trip see Waddel, *Memorials*, 478.

9 Waddel, *Memorials*, 478-479; Mayes, *History of Education*, 173-174; Sansing, *University of Mississippi*, 126-127; for a biography of Hilgard, see Hans Jenny, *E. W. Hilgard and the Birth of Modern Soil Science* (1961).

10 For the early history of Tougaloo College, see Clarice Thompson Campbell, "History of Tougaloo College," (Ph. D diss., University of Mississippi, 1970); Clarice T. Campbell and Oscar Allan Rogers, *Mississippi, The View From Tougaloo* (1979); and Mayes, *Education in Mississippi*, 259-266.

11 For a history of Rust College, see Webster B. Baker, *History of Rust college*, (1924) and Ishmell Henderson Edwards, "History of Rust College, 1866-1967," (Ph. D diss., University of Mississippi, 1993); and Mayes, *History of Education*, 266-270.

12 *Senate Journal 1886*, 501-503; Vernon Lane Wharton, *The Negro in Mississippi, 1865-1890* (1947), 250-251, 254-255; Harris, *Carpetbagger*, 343; Mayes, *History of Education*, 260-263, 267-270; see also Charles H. Wilson, Sr., *Education for Negroes in Mississippi Since 1910* (1947), 516-524; *House Journal 1896*, 30; on higher education for blacks in this period see Robert L. Jenkins, "The Development of Black Higher Education," *JMH* vol. 45,272-283.

13 James W. Garner, *Reconstruction in Mississippi* (1901), 369.

14 Ibid.; Pereyra, *Alcorn*, 123-124.

15 *Laws 1871*, 716-721; for a biographical sketch of Revels, see George A. Hewell and Margaret L. Dwight, *Mississippi Black History Makers* (1984), 7-16.

16 Harris, *Carpetbagger*, 348; Wharton, *Negro in Mississippi*, 253;

17 Melerson Guy Dunham, *Centennial History of Alcorn A.&M. College* (1971), 18 ff; Mayes, *History of Education*, 273-275; for biographical studies of Governor Ames, see Harry King Benson, "The Public Career of Adelbert Ames, 1861-1876," (Ph. D diss., University of Virginia, 1975) and Blanche Ames Ames, *Adelbert Ames 1835-1933, GeneralSoldierGovernor* (1964).

18 Governor John Marshall Stone Annual Message, *House Journal*, 1877,

19 *Laws 1878* Chapter XIX, 118-123; Mayes, *History of Education*, 275-276; for the development of coeducation at Alcorn, see W. Milan Davis, *Pushing Forward, A History of Alcorn A&MCollege and Portraits of its Successful Graduates* (1938), 27-29 and also Posey, *Alcorn, 18, 20*.

20 Waddell, *Memorials*, 480; for a biographical sketch of Reneau, see David G. Sansing, *A Place Called Mississippi* (2013), 133 and Bridget Smith Pieschel, "The History of Mississippi University for Women" on *Mississippi History Now* website.

21 Sansing, *University of Mississippi*, 136-137; on Reneau's career, see also Bridget Smith Pieschel and Stephen Robert Pieschel, *Loyal Daughters, One Hundred Years at Mississippi University for Women, 1884-1984* (1984), 4-8.

22 For the founding and early history of Mississippi State see John K. Bettersworth, *People's College, A History of Mississippi State*, (1953); after Mississippi A&M was reorganized as Mississippi State University, and during its centennial, Bettersworth published a revised and enlarged *People's University: The Centennial History of Mississippi State* (1980); in 2008 Michael Ballard published *Maroon and White, Mississippi State University, 1878-2003*.

23 For biographical information on President Lee, see Herman Hattaway, *General Stephen D. Lee* (1976); on the selection of General Lee as president, see Bettersworth, *People's College*, 42; on Lee's failure to make *Devereaux*, his Noxubee County plantation, a success see 49-50.

24 Bettersworth, *People's College*, 77-80; Hattaway, Lee, 189.

25 See *Report of Joint Select Committee Appointed to Inquire Into…the A&M College of Mississippi* (1882).

26 On the turmoil that Mississippi A&M experienced in shaping its identity in those early unsettled years, see Bettersworth, *People's University*, Chapter V "The Collegiate Course" and Chapter VI "The Cow in the Front Yard."

27 *Laws 1884*, 50-55; on the founding and early years of Industrial Institute and College, see Mayes, *History of Education*, 245-255 and Pieschel and Pieschel, *Loyal Daughters*, Chapter III "Early Friction and Factions," 21-30.

28 For President Jones' quote, see Mayes, *History of Education*, 250.

29 For President Frazer's testimony, see *House Journal 1898*, 555-570, see also Pieschel and Pieschel, *Loyal Daughters*, 38.

30 For the Joint Committee's Report of its investigation, see *House Journal 1898*, 241-244; for the testimony before the Committee, see 551-658; for the law attaching certain provisos to the Institute's appropriation, see *Laws 1898*, 41-42; for Kincannon's highly successful tenure at Industrial Institute and College, see Pieschel and Pieschel, *Loyal Daughters*, Chapter V, 40-53.

31 For details of this exchange, see Edward Mayes, *The State University, A Reply by Professor Edward Mayes to Senator James Z. George* (1887); Bettersworth, *People's University*, 99-100; Cabaniss, *University of Mississippi*, 102-103, Sansing, *University of Mississippi*, 150-152.

32 For a biography of Senator George, see Timothy B. Smith, *James Z. George, Mississippi's Great Commoner* (2011); for a biographical sketch of Mayes, see David G. Sansing, "Edward Mayes," James Lloyd, [ed.], *Lives of Mississippi Authors, 1817-1967* (1981), 327-330.

33 *Senate Journal 1886*, 504.

34 Bettersworth, *People's College*, 155; Albert Kirwan, *The Revolt of the Rednecks, Mississippi Politics: 1876-1925* (1951), 165; Bettersworth, *People's University*, 98; Mayes, *History of Education*, 231.

35 *Senate Journal 1886*, 501-503; Mayes, *History of Education*, 248; Bettersworth, *People's University*, 98; Hooker, "University of Mississippi," 132; Cabaniss, *University of Mississippi*, 104.

Chapter 4
Governing a System of Higher Education, 1900-1928

In establishing a system of higher education the Board of Trustees promised to Make Haste Slowly

Board of Trustees, 1910

Inaugurated in January 1900, Governor Andrew H. Longino was a pivotal figure in Mississippi's political history. He was the first governor elected after the Civil War who was not a Confederate veteran, and the last governor handpicked by the ruling elite that controlled the Democratic Party. In his inaugural address, Governor Longino predicted a tidal wave of industrial development and called on the legislature to change Mississippi's anti-business reputation "so that capital hunting investment [will not] pass Mississippi and go to other states offering wise, legitimate inducements." Governor Longino also hailed education as the sure remedy for what ailed Mississippi, but not traditional or classical education. He challenged the state's educational leadership "to test and prove the wisdom" of industrial education and he asked the legislature to establish a school of technology at "the Agricultural College" to provide skilled managers for the cotton mills that had been established in Mississippi during the 1880s.[1]

Governor Longino's reference to Mississippi A&M as the "Agricultural College" is significant. Mississippi's land grant institution had become a liberal arts college that provided some agricultural instruction. Industrial education at Mississippi A&M was virtually nonexistent, and in 1896, and again in 1898, President Stephen D. Lee and the Board of Trustees petitioned the legislature to establish a textile school. By 1900, the legislature was more amenable to industrial development, and during the first session in the new century the legislature established a textile school at Starkville. The original appropriation proved to be so inadequate that school officials had to go up North "to beg equipment for the new department." Fortunately, "manufacturers proved to be exceedingly generous." The textile school opened in June 1901 and the old argument about academic courses in an industrial curriculum was repeated. The classicists won again and by 1907, the director of the textile school complained that over half of its curriculum consisted of liberal arts courses emphasizing "the development of the man [and] leaving as secondary the training of the machinist." The initial popularity of the school was not sustained, and by 1911 enrollment began a precipitous decline. In 1914, the textile department was closed.²

The decline in the popularity of the textile course was paralleled by an unprecedented expansion of liberal arts courses. During the first decade of the twentieth century, A&M College achieved an astonishing academic breadth under President John C. Hardy. A department of pedagogy; a summer normal school; four departments of modern languages; and several new humanities courses were added to the curriculum. In 1911, the year that marked the beginning of the enrollment decline in the textile school, Mississippi A&M's enrollment numbered 1,090. But more than half of those students were enrolled in nontechnical courses.³

Academic proliferation at A&M drew considerable criticism from Frank Burkitt, an old adversary. Burkitt, now in the state senate, renewed his complaint about wasteful duplication at Mississippi's institutions of higher learning, and claimed that Mississippi was not getting a good return on its educational investment. Burkitt cited figures indicating that the state was spending eight times more per college student than private colleges and forty times more than it was spending per student in the public schools.⁴

James K. Vardaman, who was identified with the "redneck" faction of the Democratic Party, was elected governor in the popular primary in 1903. Because blacks were not allowed to vote in the Democratic primary it was known as the "lily white primary." In his inaugural address, Governor Vardaman chastised the Agricultural College for expanding its academic curriculum and accused it of catering to the elite. But "The White Chief" reserved his bitterest diatribes for black educational institutions. "There is no need multiplying words about it," he said, "the negro will not be permitted to rise above the station which he now fills" and education "renders him unfit for the work which the white man has prescribed." The state's only obligation to blacks, according to Governor Vardaman, was to provide vocational and moral training. The legislature did not accept Vardaman's extreme view and left the black public school system intact.⁵

Although Governor Vardaman could not persuade the legislature to dismantle the black school system, he did use his executive authority to weaken the system in two instances. First, he vetoed the appropriation for the State Normal School at Holly Springs, and the institution that had trained more than 2,000 public school teachers was forced to close in 1904. In his veto message, Governor Vardaman reiterated his claim that knowledge "inspires aspirations" in blacks that endanger white supremacy.⁶

The second instance in which Vardaman sought to weaken the black school system involved Alcorn A&M College. After Governor Vardaman became chairman of the Alcorn Board of Trustees, he forced a reduction in the salaries of its academic faculty and raised the salaries of its vocational teachers. The governor's action had the "salutary effect of discouraging higher education among Negroes and insuring that the blacks remained agricultural laborers."[7]

James K. Vardaman was elected governor in 1903 largely by Mississippi's dirt farmers and day laborers and he promised them that he would drive the wealthy elite from their positions of power and privilege. Like the common people he championed, Governor Vardaman considered Ole Miss the last bastion of the old aristocracy, and he was determined to democratize it. The need to democratize Ole Miss was dramatized in 1905 when seven fraternity students who had been suspended for violating the rules governing Greek societies were readmitted and allowed to graduate. The readmission of those students angered Dean Garvin Shands of the law school and Duncan H. Chamberlain, an ardent anti-fraternity law student. In January 1906, Chamberlain published a pamphlet to inform the "common people" of Mississippi that their University was still catering to "the so called upper classes" and he accused Chancellor Robert Fulton of being partial to fraternity boys. Since 1897, when the Greek societies published the first annual and named it *Ole Miss,* the University of Mississippi has also been identified as Ole Miss.[8]

To clear away rumor from fact, Chancellor Fulton asked the legislature to investigate the charges. Acting on his request a legislative committee conducted an investigation that completely exonerated Fulton. Three committee members, however, presented a minority report critical of Fulton and asked the Board of Trustees to conduct its own investigation. After the publication of Chamberlain's pamphlet and the legislature's investigation, which some said was stacked in Fulton's favor, Governor Vardaman was convinced that the University needed new leadership. It would not be easy for Vardaman to remove Fulton. He had been at the University for nearly forty years and he was the brother-in-law of Congressman John Sharp Williams, Vardaman's opponent in the upcoming United States Senate election. Vardaman's political adversaries could claim that Fulton's dismissal was due to factional politics. Nevertheless, when Vardaman appointed new board members in 1906, he made certain that they would vote to dismiss Chancellor Fulton.[9]

For several weeks prior to the June board meeting, there was speculation that Chancellor Fulton would be dismissed if he did not voluntarily resign. The chancellor vowed not to resign. A few days before the meeting, Fulton was convinced by his supporters on the board that he did not have enough votes to survive, and he tendered his resignation. Chancellor Fulton said he would not continue to serve a board "swayed by the will of their master, Vardaman," and he declined the board's offer of the chair of astronomy.[10]

Chancellor Fulton was not the only casualty of that June 1906 board meeting.

Dean Garvin Shands was also forced to resign, largely at the insistence of Judge Robert Powell, one of Vardaman's new board appointees. Judge Powell's son was one of the seven students originally expelled in 1905. The judge personally blamed Dean Shands and was determined to "drive" him from the University. The board reduced Dean Shands' salary by $400 in a move calculated to induce his resignation.[11]

Removal of Chancellor Fulton and Dean Shands, and the long delay in finding a replacement for Fulton, convinced a large segment of Mississippi's leadership that some way must be found to shield the institutions of higher learning from factional politics. There was also increasing popular support for greater coordination among the state colleges and the elimination of costly duplication. Under those circumstances, and with the near unanimous consent of the state's educational leadership, the legislature abolished the four existing college boards in 1910 and established a central Board of Trustees. To keep the colleges out of politics, and politics out of the colleges, elected officials were prohibited from serving on the new Board of Trustees. The central board governed the state university, Alcorn A&M, Mississippi A&M, and the Industrial Institute and College. The central board, as the new board was sometimes called, did not govern the Mississippi Normal School that was established in 1910 at Hattiesburg or Delta State Teachers College when it opened at Cleveland in 1924. The two teachers' colleges were governed by separate boards until 1932 when the legislature consolidated the three existing boards.[12]

The new Board of Trustees, which was composed primarily of businessmen, met for the first time in July 1910 and pledged to meet its responsibility with an "openness of mind." Its decisions would be based on an assessment of Mississippi's immediate and long range educational needs. The board announced that it would reorganize the four separate institutions into a coordinated state system of higher education. There would be many changes, and some might appear to be radical. The board reassured the people of Mississippi that it would "make haste slowly."[13]

Businessmen who governed the state's institutions of higher learning in 1910 recognized the link between Mississippi's economic progress and its educational system, and that relationship was the subject of the first speech by James Sexton, the consolidated board's first and only president. In a speech at Ole Miss, Sexton heralded the creation of the unified board as a "mile post in the educational history of our state" and made an impassioned plea for a coordinated system of public education extending from the elementary level up to the state university. A coordinated system, he asserted, was essential for the development of Mississippi's economic resources. Duplication and rivalry among the state's collegiate institutions had impeded Mississippi's economic development, and Sexton called on college officials to "banish forever the puerile idea" that there is "any sort of rivalry" between the University and other state colleges. "But," he quickly added, "it is preeminently the mission of the University to set the pace for all our educational institutions."[14]

Reorganization of Mississippi's governing boards and the effort to coordinate the state's colleges into a system of higher education paralleled a national trend that Laurence Veysey identified as "a season of assessment." Veysey explained: "The years 1908, 1909, and 1910 witnessed the widest flurry of debate about the aims of higher education ever to occur so far in the United States. The existence of the debate, which soon became widely spread throughout the general magazines, provided one of the signs that an era of academic pioneering had come to an end. This was a season when men drew back and took stock."[15]

It can only be wondered if Mississippi's new Board of Trustees, which came into being during that "season of assessment," could have achieved the great promise that its first efforts presaged. After only two years, the nonpolitical board would be superseded and the provision that excluded elected officials from serving on the board would be repealed. In January 1912, Frank Burkitt introduced a bill to repeal the 1910 statute, and many other public officials asserted that the state's collegiate institutions should not be controlled by "designing school men" who were not responsible to the taxpayer or subject to the popular will. The 1912 statute completely reorganized the Board of Trustees and reinstated the governor as *ex officio* president.[16]

While the legislature was debating the various bills to reorganize the governing board in 1912, William A. Ellis of Carthage introduced a resolution to study the feasibility of consolidating the University of Mississippi and the Agricultural College. It was clear to Ellis that Mississippi's long term interests would be better served by a system of higher education rather than several autonomous and rival institutions. Although it would not require a consolidation, only a consideration of that possibility, Ellis' resolution was defeated.[17]

There were several factors that contributed to the 1912 law reorganizing the board and reinstating the governor as *ex officio* president. The most important factor was the long-standing presumption, especially among members of the legislature, that the governor was the head of the state's educational institutions in the same way that he was head of the state militia. That presumption is illustrated by a legislative resolution authorizing a special visitation of the state colleges. Heading the delegation, in the words of the resolution, would be "Governor Edmund F. Noel, as chairman of the state's educational institutions." That presumption was held by the senate as well. An example of that presumption is the resolution to abolish coeducation at the University of Mississippi that was ruled out of order by the chairman of the senate because "the Governor had not recommended the subject matter."[18]

Another factor in the 1912 reorganization was the lingering controversy involving Chancellor Andrew Kincannon. There had been several accusations against University officials including fiscal mismanagement, football recruiting violations, and sexual improprieties. The Kincannon controversy was cited by some of the state's leading politicians as a justification for reasserting the state's official authority over its institutions of higher learning. Although a legislative committee exonerated Chancellor Kincannon and other university officials, rumors and innuendos continued to plague his administration and he resigned in 1914 because, "I was unwilling for the school to become a political chattel." Some of Chancellor Kincannon's most serious problems stemmed from athletics. In his centennial history of the University of Mississippi Professor Cabaniss writes, "There was acute dissension within the faculty growing out of a feeling that disproportionate emphasis was being placed on athletics." Ole Miss was suspended from the Southern Intercollegiate Athletic Association in 1914 for illegal aid to athletes.[19]

Two years after Chancellor Kincannon's resignation a similar situation occurred at Mississippi A&M. President George R. Hightower, "a Governor Brewer appointee," had become unpopular after four years in office. The movement to dismiss Hightower found favor with Governor Theodore G. Bilbo who was in his first term as governor from 1916 to 1920. During the 1915 campaign "Bilbo had made a statement that his first act would be to 'kick out' Hightower, for which act he had reserved a 'special pair of boots.'" With the near unanimous consent of the Board of Trustees Governor Bilbo removed President Hightower. Editor Fred Sullens of the *Jackson Daily News* wrote that President Hightower's removal was unfortunate but necessary.[20]

Chancellor Kincannon's resignation and President Hightower's dismissal prompted another public outcry about politics and the governance of higher education. The *Itta Bena Times* declared: "It is time to quit playing politics in the management of institutions of higher learning. We must get a better faculty [and] provide them with a sense of security and stability." Judge Walter Clark of Clarksdale agreed that it was time to quit playing politics at Ole Miss and A&M and issued a challenge to the friends of both institutions:

> It seems to me that the time is ripe for those men who have attended the University of Mississippi and the Agricultural and Mechanical College at Starkville to end the reign of politics in these two institutions.... There are enough Oxford and Starkville men in Mississippi with sufficient brains and influence forcibly to tear these schools out of the grasp of the politician.[21]

Although Judge Clark made no reference to the Industrial Institute and College in his appeal to end to the "reign of politics" in higher education, he should have.

When Lee Russell ran for governor in 1919 he sought the endorsement of its president, Henry Whitfield, who declined to support Russell, and actively campaigned for his opponent. Russell was elected in 1919. He fired Whitfield in 1920. In his fine biography of Whitfield, Bill Baker records the fascinating story of a college president who was fired in 1920, but was elected governor in 1923.²²

The effort to end the reign of politics, and to consolidate some of Mississippi's institutions of higher learning, seemed to be a lost cause. But Mississippians love lost causes, and the governance of higher education was a prominent issue in the 1920 legislative session. Several bills to restructure the governance of higher education were introduced in the 1920 session. The most ambitious measure was proposed by George L. Sheldon, a representative from Washington County. Sheldon's bill would consolidate the University of Mississippi, the Agricultural College, and the Industrial Institute into one institution, and would be located in Jackson. The Industrial Institute and College would be continued in Columbus as a junior college for women.²³

Senator Julius C. Zeller of Yazoo County was the bill's floor leader in the senate, and the press usually referred to the measure as the Sheldon-Zeller Bill. After the bill was introduced, the legislature received petitions from alumni of all three institutions opposing the consolidation plan. But there were many who favored it. Governor Bilbo, whose first term was just ending, supported the consolidation and the *Jackson Daily News* reported that the new governor, Lee Russell, and House Speaker Mike Conner, also favored the bill.²⁴

Senator Zeller met with a group of Jackson citizens on January 21, 1920 to discuss the advantages of consolidating the three institutions at Jackson. Zeller explained that the physical plant at Ole Miss was in deplorable condition and that university officials had requested $700,000 for emergency repair and expansion. Mississippi A&M and the Industrial Institute and College at Columbus had also made urgent requests for repair and renovation, and the legislature was considering a special $2,000,000 appropriation for the three institutions. It would be wiser to spend that money on one new consolidated university, Zeller said, than to repair old, worn-out buildings. Zeller quickly added that consolidation should not be based on considerations of brick and mortar alone: "This is the psychological moment for the legislature to realize that if we are ever to have a great university, an institution that will compare favorably with universities in other states, we must build anew, locate the university at a center of population, broaden the scope of its work, and make it a University in something more than a name."²⁵

As convincing as Zeller's argument was, there was little popular support for consolidation outside of Jackson, and the Sheldon-Zeller bill was not enacted. After that measure was defeated several other options were considered. Some legislators opposed consolidation, but favored moving the University to Jackson. To get that option before the legislature Lamar Williams of Newton County introduced "An Act to move the University of Mississippi...to the city of Jackson." When Williams' bill got to the floor for debate, Representative Buz M. Walker, Jr., the son of Buz M. Walker, Sr., the Dean of the School of Engineering and future president of Mississippi A&M, offered an amendment to abolish the school of engineering at the University and transfer all engineering courses to Mississippi A&M. Walker's amendment was tabled and the bill to move the state university to Jackson was defeated by a vote of eighty-two to thirty-seven.[26]

Ironically, the only change that resulted from all of that legislative maneuvering was a change in name. During the debate prompted by the consolidation bill, President Henry Whitfield invited the legislature to visit the Industrial Institute and College. After their visit the lawmakers voted to keep the school independent and autonomous, and upgraded its name to Mississippi State College for Women.[27]

Although thwarted in 1920, the proponents of reform did not abandon their effort to end the rule of politics in the governance of higher education. In 1922 the joint legislative committee on the university and colleges visited each state institution of higher learning and found the campuses in varying stages of ill-repair. After expressing its concern about the physical condition of the campuses, the committee spoke to the issue of politics and inveighed against its disruptive effects:

> If the Czar of Russia and the Kaiser of Germany could pursue a policy of hands off when it came to their university professors, then surely we can observe this rule.

What the Czar and the Kaiser could do, Mississippi governors could not, or would not do, and during political campaigns gubernatorial candidates invariably solicited the support of college presidents and faculty.[28]

The 1923 governor's race illustrates the link between politics and academics and documents its consequences. When Henry L. Whitfield, the former president of Mississippi State College for Women, ran for governor against Theodore G. Bilbo in 1923, the Board of Trustees made a special effort to keep the colleges out of politics and deluded themselves into thinking that they had. Ambrose B. Schauber, the secretary of the Board of Trustees, wrote to Governor Lee Russell on July 23, 1923:

> The Board of Trustees adopted a policy some time ago of keeping the schools out of politics...and I am glad to be able to report that this policy of the Board of Trustees has been adhered to by everyone connected with these institutions.

Secretary Schauber's statement is incredible, given that from the outset of that campaign the institutions of higher learning were deeply entangled in the contest.

Henry Whitfield, who was running for governor, sought and secured the public endorsement of President Joseph Cook of the Mississippi State Teachers College at Hattiesburg, and appointed Harry Bryan, the son-in-law of Vice-Chancellor Alfred Hume of the University, as his state campaign manager. Whitfield also had the active support of the MSCW alumnae association. Theodore Bilbo, like Whitfield, had sought and received the public endorsement of several college officials including Ole Miss Chancellor Joseph Neely Powers.[29]

Henry Whitfield was elected in 1923 and his victory meant that Joseph Neely Powers would be dismissed as chancellor of the University. Powers and Whitfield had been adversaries since the early 1900s when both men had served as the elected state superintendent of education. At the June 1924 board meeting a motion was made to reelect Chancellor Powers. Governor Whitfield's three appointees, along with Willard F. Bond, the State Superintendent of Education and an old ally of Whitfield, voted no. The four carry over board members voted yes. Governor Whitfield broke the tie by voting to dismiss Chancellor Powers. A motion was then made to elect Alfred Hume chancellor. That motion also produced a tie vote and Governor Whitfield again broke the tie by voting to appoint Hume, the father-in-law of his campaign manager. Six years later, when Bilbo gained control of the Board of Trustees, Hume was removed and Powers was reinstated.[30]

His own political entanglements notwithstanding, Governor Whitfield was an enlightened governor whose progressive leadership was cut short by his death in 1927. During the 1923 campaign Whitfield had addressed the problems of rural unemployment and the alarming increase of racial violence. Once in office he embraced a broad legislative program including better mental health care, tax reform, industrial development, expanded vocational training, and improvement in the quality of life for Mississippi's black citizens.[31]

Whitfield's moderate position on race received a generally favorable response and even praise from some of the state press. In commenting on Whitfield's pledge to be the governor of all the people, including blacks, the *Jackson Daily News* admitted: "We all know...that we have not given the negro a square deal, and it is gratifying to know that we have a governor endowed with the courage to speak out and tell the truth about it." The Committee of One Hundred, an organization of leading black citizens, also praised the governor for his courageous stand.[32]

Governor Whitfield's determination to mollify race relations was only one part of his broader plan to reorder the state's priorities. Whitfield realized that Mississippi's economic development was linked to its educational system and it was obvious to him that the system needed fundamental reform. The governor was especially concerned that the state university had not broadened its service role or geared its research efforts toward solving some of the state's most pressing problems. Governor Whitfield went to Oxford and personally appealed to University officials to form an alliance with the state of Mississippi, as the University of Wisconsin had done with the state of Wisconsin. The pragmatic relationship between a state and a state university was epitomized in Wisconsin and was known as the "Wisconsin Idea." Governor Whitfield envisioned that same kind of relationship between Mississippi and its institutions of higher learning and soon after his inauguration he moved toward making that goal a reality. In the fall of 1924 Governor Whitfield took a delegation of farmers, bankers, businessmen, and educators on a two week trip to Wisconsin to study the "Wisconsin Idea." That trip convinced the state's business leaders that a similar program could be implemented in Mississippi and they returned with a new-found faith in the state's economic future. While the business community, in cooperation with the legislature, was designing a strategy for industrial development, Governor Whitfield arranged for a University of Wisconsin consulting team to conduct a comprehensive study of Mississippi's entire educational system. The study was conducted under the supervision of Professor Michael V. O'Shea and it was the first professional appraisal of Mississippi's institutions of higher learning. His report, known as the O'Shea Study, was published in 1927.[33]

In its preamble the O'Shea Study applauded the state's leadership for acknowledging "that their prosperity individually and as a state depends upon 'universal education.'" Mississippi's institutions of higher learning, however, according to the study, "had resisted modernization and were clinging to the 'Genteel Tradition' [that] was in vogue throughout our country fifty years ago." The report also noted that "one frequently hears the phrase, 'We plan our courses so as to develop character in our young people,'" but rarely finds a curriculum designed to "train young people to develop the agricultural, industrial, economic, and human resources of Mississippi." That assessment was followed by a warning, and a prediction that came true: "If the higher institutions do not modify their program in view of the special needs of Mississippi, it may easily happen that the state will be seriously drained of its superior young men and women, educating them for other states where they stand a chance of finding employment."[34]

Consequently, O'Shea recommended that Mississippi's system of higher education be thoroughly reorganized and restructured. Specifically, he recommended the establishment of a single State Board of Education with authority over the public schools and the institutions of higher learning, the appointment of a commissioner of higher education, and the merger of the three white institutions of higher learning into one University of Mississippi. The three separate campuses could be maintained but each would be assigned and limited to specific degree programs. The two teachers colleges, at Hattiesburg and Cleveland, which had greatly expanded their liberal arts curriculum, would also be continued and their degree programs would be limited to teacher education. O'Shea stated that he had not conducted a study of Alcorn A&M and his report included few recommendations about higher education for blacks.[35]

The O'Shea Study singled out the University of Mississippi for special criticism and several specific recommendations. The O'Shea staff recommended a revision of the University's curriculum; more research activity directed toward solving Mississippi's social and economic problems; and higher academic standards for the faculty. Of the three recommendations, according to the O'Shea Study, faculty development should be the University's top priority. "The University of Mississippi can render service to the state much more effectively," the report concluded, "by building up its faculty than by expanding its physical plant."[36]

In 1927, the year the O'Shea Study was published, Theodore G. Bilbo was elected governor for a second term. In his second inaugural address Bilbo referenced the O'Shea Study and pledged to implement its recommendations. Governor Bilbo's determination to reform and improve the institutions of higher learning lingers in Mississippi's historical memory as a great myth that is at variance with historical fact.

Footnotes Chapter 4

1 For Governor Longino's Inaugural see McArthur, *Inaugural Addresses*, 11-19.

2 Bettersworth, *People's University, see* Chapter VII, "Toward Engineering," 81-91 and 117-121.

3 Ibid., 109, 110-151.

4 Albert Kirwan, *Revolt of the Rednecks*, 165-166; Bettersworth, *People's University,* 133.

5 Kirwan, *Revolt of the Rednecks,*, 145-146; see Vardaman's inaugural address in McArthur, *Inaugural Addresses*, 29-30.

6 William F. Holmes, *The White Chief, James Kimble Vardaman* (1970), 121-122; on black education during the Jim Crow era see Neil McMillen, *Dark Journey, Black Mississippians in the Age of Jim Crow* (1989), Chapter 3 "Education: The Mere Faint Gesture," 72-111.

7 Holmes, *Vardaman*, 182.

8 Ibid., 167-176; Sansing, *University of Mississippi*, 178-181, 168-169; *Historical Catalogue, 1849-1909*, 78.

9 Holmes, *Vardaman*, 172-174.

10 Ibid, 174-176; Hooker, "University of Mississippi," 165-167.

11 Holmes, *Vardaman*, 174.

12 *Laws 1910*, 105-109. One trustee was designated the LaBauve Trustee to superintend a scholarship fund at the University of Mississippi established by Felix LaBauve for orphan boys from DeSoto County. That special trustee was sometimes identified as the "Ole Miss Trustee" and remained a controversial issue until the trustee was finally abolished in 1987.

13 Board of Trustees, State Institutions of Higher Learning, *First Biennial Report*, 5, 16, 44-45; for a discussion of the vocational makeup of college boards see W. H. Cowley, *Presidents, Professors, and Trustees: The Evolution of American Academic Government* (1980); on the changing character of the American college and university during the early twentieth century see David O. Levine, *The American College and the Culture of Aspiration, 1915-1940* (1986) especially Chapter 3, "Business Goes to the Colleges," 45-68.

14 Sexton's speech is printed in *Mississippi School Journal* (October, 1910), 1-12.

15 Laurence Veysey, *The Emergence of the American University* (1965), 252.

16 *Laws 1912*, 179-181; *Senate Journal 1912*, 223, 232, 240, 480.

17 *Senate Journal 1912*, 379, 664, 706.

18 Bettersworth, in *People's University*, writes, "Presidents and governors went in together and out together," 157. When President Robert C. Cook arrived at Mississippi Southern College in Hattiesburg in 1945 faculty members were still introducing themselves as a "Governor Bilbo appointee," or a "Governor Conner appointee," or a "Governor Johnson appointee;" see Robert C. Cook Interview, Oral History Collection, University of Southern Mississippi.

19 *Senate Journal 1912*, 746-747; Cabaniss, *University of Mississippi*, 127; see also Hooker, "University of Mississippi," 214-215.

20 Bettersworth, *People's University*, 178; *Jackson Daily News*, July 2, 1916.

21 *Itta Bena Times* and Memphis *Commercial Appeal*, undated clippings in Institutions of Higher Learning Subject File, MDAH.

22 Bill Baker, *Catch the Vision, The Life of Henry L. Whitfield* (1974), 73-74; see Pieschel and Pieschel, *Loyal Daughters*, Chapter VI, "Whitfield: Pragmatic Educator and Statesman," 55-72.

23 *House Journal 1920*, 367, 384, 1216, 1228, 1371; *Senate Journal 1920*, 466-467; *Jackson Daily News*, January 21, 22, 23, 25, 1920.

24 *Jackson Daily News*, January 23, 1920.

25 Ibid.; see also Sansing, *University of Mississippi*, 200-201, 221.

26 *House Journal 1920*, 1374, 1029, 1217, 1235, 1505, 1542, 1542, 1592-1593.

27 Ibid, 231, 324, 488; Baker, *Whitfield*, 71-73; *Jackson Daily News*, January 21, 1920.

28 *Senate Journal 1922*, 591-592; *Minutes*, July 23, 1923.

29 Baker, *Whitfield*, 81, 82, 89, 92; Hardy Poindexter Graham, "Bilbo and the University of Mississippi, 1928-1932," (M.A. thesis, University of Mississippi, 1965), 32; Sansing, *University of Mississippi*, 211-212.

30 Hooker, "University of Mississippi," 251, 255-256; for biographical information on Alfred Hume see Francis Egger Watson, "Dr. Alfred Hume: His Leadership as Vice Chancellor, Acting Chancellor, and Chancellor of the University of Mississippi 1905-1945," (Ph. D diss., University of Mississippi, 1987), 13-23.

31 Baker, *Whitfield*, see Chapter 3, "Governor of Mississippi, 78-116.

32 Ibid.

33 Michael V. O'Shea, *Public Education in Mississippi* (1927); Governor Henry L. Whitfield, *Know Mississippi, A Syllabus on Present Conditions in Mississippi* (n.p. n.d), see especially the sections on public schools, 21-36 and higher education, 42-53; Baker, *Whitfield*, 111.

34 O'Shea Study, 200-01, 325-35, 348, 351.

35 Ibid, 32-34, 214.

36 Ibid, 221-223.

Chapter 5
The Bilbo Purge, 1928-1932

But I was looking fifty years ahead for Mississippi.
Governor Theodore G. Bilbo

When the O'Shea Study was published in June 1927, Mississippi was in the midst of a heated political campaign between Theodore Bilbo and Dennis Murphree. The state's institutions of higher learning, as usual, were in the thick of the fray, and as the campaign progressed Bilbo became increasingly troubled by the political involvement of college officials and board members. President J. C. Fant of MSCW had given a glowing introduction of Dennis Murphree at a special student assembly that left little doubt about his personal preference for governor. MSCW alumni made no effort to conceal their support for Murphree. Various alumni groups bought newspaper advertisements and wrote letters on his behalf. Two members of the College Board, and the wife of a former board member, who had ties to MSCW, were members of Murphree's state campaign committee. The opposition to Bilbo among MSCW supporters stemmed in large measure from his support of the Sheldon-Zeller bill in 1920. There was also open opposition to Bilbo among the staff and alumni at Mississippi A&M College and State Teachers College at Hattiesburg. Bilbo was made aware of that political involvement by his own partisans at those institutions.[1]

It was the opposition of Ole Miss officials, however, that most troubled that seasoned veteran of six campaigns. Robert Farley, a young law professor, wrote letters to friends and alumni urging them to work for Bilbo's defeat. "A vote for Bilbo is a vote against Chancellor Hume," Farley explained. Farley's conjecture was based on rumors that Bilbo, if elected, would fire Chancellor Hume and reinstate his old friend Joseph Neely Powers, who had been fired four years earlier by Governor Whitfield. The fact that Powers was campaigning for Bilbo, and had endorsed his populist promise of free textbooks, lent credence to Farley's assumption. When Bilbo learned of Farley's letters, he asked Chancellor Hume to reprimand Farley and instruct him to quit the campaign against him. Chancellor Hume refused to do so, telling Bilbo that Farley's private political opinions did not come under his jurisdiction and he would not intervene.[2]

There were several other University officials who campaigned against Bilbo, including William Hemingway, the former Mayor of Jackson and a professor of law, who openly ridiculed Bilbo and his redneck politics in his law classes. Thomas Turner and other Bilbo partisans kept records on University personnel who campaigned against him and passed that information on to the governor. Turner later served on the Board of Trustees of State Institutions of Higher Learning from 1964 to 1976.[3]

Bilbo was embittered by the politics of Ole Miss officials, and their opposition to his populist platform was proof, in his mind at least, that the University was still catering to Mississippi's old aristocracy. Like his predecessor Henry Whitfield and some other southern governors, Huey Long of Louisiana in particular, Bilbo looked to the state university as a catalyst in the solution of the state's social and economic problems. As Governor Whitfield and Michael O'Shea had found, Ole Miss was still under the sway of the "Genteel Tradition" and the notion that a university should train the mind and build character. The success of Bilbo's populist platform of economic development would, in some important aspects, depend upon a progressive, problem solving state university. Bilbo was convinced that Ole Miss as it existed in 1927, an isolated liberal arts college in poor repair, in a "sylvan exile" could contribute little to Mississippi's "progress and future glory." He now had the findings of the O'Shea Study as he began to formulate his plan to restructure Mississippi's system of higher education during the political canvas of 1927.[4]

As the reorganization plan was being formulated, bits and pieces of it leaked to the press. One version of the plan called for sweeping changes in the system's leadership and rumors ran amok about who would be dismissed. Another feature of Bilbo's plan that became the subject of increasing speculation was the relocation of the University to Jackson. The possibility of moving Ole Miss to Jackson first surfaced around 1900, again soon after the establishment of the central board in 1910, and again in 1920. Some legislative leaders had considered the relocation of the University to be such a likely possibility that they were reluctant to build up the Oxford campus. In 1927, "the University was slowly dying of neglect, and drastic measures were necessary if the institution was to be revitalized"[5]

As the question of moving the University to Jackson became increasingly the subject of public discussion, the tone of that discussion became increasingly emotional and sentimental. In December 1927, Chancellor Alfred Hume issued a public statement opposing the relocation of the University. Many Mississippians of that era had been baptized in "the blood of the lost cause" and Chancellor Hume played upon those precious memories with great skill and success:

> The University of Mississippi is rich in memories and memorials and a noble history.... The memorial window in the old library

erected in loving memory of the University Grays, the Confederate monument nearby, and the Confederate soldiers' cemetery a little farther removed are as sacred as any ancient shrine, alter, or temple. Instead of moving the University away that it might be a little easier to reach, ought not the people of Mississippi to look upon a visit here as a holy pilgrimage.[6]

Governor Bilbo was inaugurated for his second term on January 17, 1928. His inaugural address was well crafted and even editor Fred Sullens of the *Jackson Daily News*, one of Bilbo's bitterest critics, gave grudging due. Sullens wrote that Bilbo's inaugural was one of "the ablest messages...in the memory of this writer." Other papers, even some that had opposed his election, praised his inaugural address, though many expressed reservations about the cost of his agenda, which was estimated at one hundred million dollars.[7]

The high cost of Bilbo's legislative program triggered a conditioned response from a powerful coalition known as the "low pressure" faction of the Democratic Party. The low pressure faction was composed of fiscal conservatives who were dedicated to the proposition of low taxes and economy in government. Bilbo represented the populist or redneck faction, which outnumbered the low pressure group but enjoyed little legislative success because it was out maneuvered by the crafty conservatives who controlled both houses of the legislature. The low pressure faction was stunned by the visionary and costly proposals in Governor Bilbo's inaugural and they, with help from the Great Depression, ultimately defeated his legislative program.

Bilbo's inaugural address embraced a wide range of reforms and other programs that he considered essential to Mississippi's social and economic development. He reiterated his campaign proposal for free textbooks; a modern mental hospital; two charity hospitals; a separate correctional facility for young inmates; and a massive highway program. But it was his proposal to reorganize and restructure the governance of higher education that created the firestorm.

After citing some of the O'Shea Study's recommendations, Governor Bilbo proposed sweeping changes in the governance of higher education. One of his priorities was the establishment of an eight member central governing board, one from each of the eight congressional districts, who would serve eight year staggered terms with one member going off the board each year "so that no governor could appoint the majority of said board." The governor also recommended a five member "largely advisory" board for each of the six institutions of higher learning, who would serve four year terms. To coordinate the governance of higher education Governor Bilbo recommended the establishment of a "director of higher education [who would be] placed in charge of all institutions of college rank."

To these recommendations, Bilbo proposed the establishment of what he called "The Greater University of Mississippi" at Jackson:

> If I were called upon to name the one thing that would do more to develop Mississippi and bring to her the highest degree of progress and future glory than anything else, I would not hesitate in saying that the moving of the University of Mississippi to the capital city of Jackson and the building and equipment of a twelve or fifteen million dollar institution would be that thing.[8]

The day after Bilbo was inaugurated, Senator Linton Glover North introduced a resolution to relocate the University of Mississippi to Jackson. Senator North was a native of Vicksburg, a graduate of Mississippi A&M College and, according to the *Jackson Daily News*, was "an upstanding, progressive young man" who was motivated by "the sole hope of building a bigger and better University." The *Daily News* reminded its readers that Senator Julius Zeller had recommended the establishment of one consolidated university in Jackson eight years earlier. "But the legislature," said the *Daily News*, "lacked the largeness of vision to see it."[9]

Jackson business leaders heartily endorsed the relocation of the state university, but they had some reservation about the twelve to fifteen million dollar cost of the new institution. Governor Bilbo's response to their concern is an indication of just how committed he was to the establishment of a great university:

> I fully understand that the proposal suggested in my inaugural address is a big one, but I was looking fifty years ahead for Mississippi.... [T]he start could be made in a smaller way, but the plans must be made for the distant future.[10]

While the populist governor and the Jackson plutocrats were forming what some may have considered an unholy alliance, Chancellor Hume was plotting to keep Ole Miss at Oxford. His strategy, based not on reason but sentiment, appealed to sense of place and evoked the memory of the Lost Cause. Chancellor Hume expressed that sentiment in an address to the legislature:

> Gentlemen, you may move the University of Mississippi...You may uproot it from the hallowed ground on which it has stood for eighty years. You may take it from these surroundings that have become dear to the thousands who have gone from its doors. But, gentlemen, don't call it Ole Miss.[11]

The legislature was stirred by the chancellor's rhetoric and voted 109 to 9 to leave Ole Miss at Oxford. Two weeks later Governor Bilbo addressed a joint session and conceded that the University would not be relocated. He then entreated the lawmakers to build a Greater University at Oxford and asked for a special appropriation of five million dollars for new buildings. He also urged the legislature to

Chapter 5 — The Bilbo Purge, 1928-1932

build hard surface roads from various points in the state to Oxford to make Ole Miss more accessible.[12]

Bilbo's entreaties went unheeded and the legislature appropriated only 1.5 million dollars. The governor was irked by that paltry appropriation, but he was more upset with the Board of Trustees and Chancellor Hume for not asking for more. In 1927, Chancellor Hume had asked for $165,000 for capital improvements and, in spite of the dire needs of the University, he requested only $265,000 in 1928.[13]

As concerned as Governor Bilbo was about the University's physical condition, he was even more concerned about its academic programs that had come under heavy criticism in the past few years. In 1927, the Ole Miss law school lost its accreditation and the University's medical school was placed on probation. Two years later, the Southern Association of Colleges and Schools found that the University's general academic program did not meet several of its standards. The Southern Association singled out the faculty for special criticism and noted that a "large proportion" of the faculty had taken their degrees at the University. SACS did not rescind the University's accreditation but recommended that Chancellor Hume eliminate those deficiencies as soon as possible.[14]

That $1,500,000 appropriation that Bilbo secured in 1928 enabled Chancellor Hume to remedy some of the most glaring deficiencies and infused the University with new vigor. Chancellor Hume reported that a "transformation is being wrought." Hoping to capitalize on the expansive spirit of that transformation, a department chairman went to Chancellor Hume with a request to buy "the back issues of an important professional journal" at a cost of $125. According to procedures then in place, all library purchases were personally approved by the chancellor. In spite of the fact that part of the special appropriation was slated for library improvements, Chancellor Hume denied the professor's request. Chancellor Hume told the department chairman that he "found it difficult to persuade the students to read the textbook, much less outside reading assignments [and] saw no reason why $125 should be spent on old periodicals."[15]

When Chancellor Hume announced that the University would use some of the 1928 appropriation for the purchase of new steel library shelves, the *Mississippian* proclaimed "Let's first get a Library." W. A. Lomax, the student editor, ridiculed the library's holdings in philosophy, science, and mathematics, most of which, he said, had either been "donated [or] bought at auctions." If a book "even hints at disturbing the established political, social, or religious questions of the day, it is not on the University Library shelves" and that, Lomax asserted, should "not be the case in a great University, the alleged home of free thought."[16]

It was obvious to Governor Bilbo that Ole Miss was not a great university in

1928; it was not even a good university, and he was convinced that under Chancellor Hume it would not become one. Known fondly as "Little Allie," Chancellor Hume was perhaps the most popular and beloved chancellor in the institution's history. In 1930 he was sixty-four years old and had been at the University forty years. Hume was a devout Presbyterian, and when he assumed the office of chancellor in 1924, he announced the singular goal of his administration:

> My greatest aspiration for the present administration is...not that we excel in scholarship and athletics...I am hoping that it may be truthfully said that it was characterized by the exalting of character, by putting the emphasis on things moral, by stressing religious and spiritual values.[17]

Chancellor Hume's administrative policies were an extension of his personal faith and he cloaked the University in a religious atmosphere. Students were not allowed to smoke, drink, dance, wear shorts on campus, or play tennis on Sunday and were required to attend daily chapel services. Ole Miss was often called, in jest, "Hume's Presbyterian University." Michael O'Shea's pointed criticism that Mississippi institutions of higher learning planned their "courses so as to develop character" was probably directed at the University.[18]

Chancellor Hume, according to Hardy Poindexter Graham, also embraced "the University's traditional role" as the institution devoted primarily to the needs of the upper classes of Mississippi society. But Governor Bilbo was determined that the University of Mississippi would not remain a liberal arts academy or a provincial university hidden away in the hills of northeast Mississippi. He would transform the University if he could not relocate it.[19]

In June 1928, Bilbo announced his intention to replace Chancellor Hume if he could persuade the Board of Trustees to do so. The board rejected Governor Bilbo's recommendation, and Hume was reelected. Governor Bilbo was successful, however, in persuading the board that governed the State Teachers College at Hattiesburg to dismiss Joseph Anderson Cook, the school's first and only president. President Cook had come under heavy fire in recent years from former students, alumni, and public school teachers who believed that his administrative philosophy was antiquated. He routinely locked the gates to the campus at twilight and movement on and off the campus after dark was restricted. Many professional and business leaders in Mississippi's rapidly growing coastal region envisioned a much broader role and scope for the State Teachers College and they were doubtful that Cook, who was then sixty-five years old, had either the vision or the vigor to develop its enormous potential. Governor Bilbo agreed with that assessment and recommended that the board replace him with a younger, more progressive administrator. The board initially refused to dismiss President Cook, but when Robert E. Lee

Sutherland resigned from the board, his replacement voted not to renew President Cook's contract. Claude Bennett, the superintendent of Biloxi city schools, replaced President Cook in October 1928.[20]

Governor Bilbo renewed his effort to remove Chancellor Hume in 1929, and he was more convinced than ever that Hume was "temperamentally unfit" to be chancellor of a modern comprehensive state university. The incident that strengthened his resolve was Hume's dismissal of the editors of the college yearbook. Chancellor Hume decreed that some of the yearbook's poetry and puns were "libelous slurs at girlhood and womanhood" and he impounded the annual, expelled the editors, and established a board of control to censor future student publications.[21]

The expulsion was given extensive press coverage and Hume came under heavy criticism for the arbitrary manner in which he handled the entire affair, and was under intense pressure to reinstate the students. Eventually, Chancellor Hume did reinstate one of them but denied that he had done so under pressure from the board or anyone else. Chancellor Hume explained that his reinstatement of the student was an "act of free grace" and that he had meted out "mercy not justice" because the student had come to him as a "penitent child or sinner." Hume proclaimed that he would never compromise a principle because, in an obvious reference to Bilbo's characterization of him, he was "temperamentally unfit" for that sort of thing.[22]

In his 1929 report to the Board of Trustees, Chancellor Hume explained the expulsion of the two students and addressed the larger issue of freedom of thought at a university. In most cases, he conceded, faculty members should be given the right to express their opinions. "[But] occasionally freaks are found," he said, "who prove exceptions to the rule." Academic freedom may sometimes be academic nonsense, the chancellor added, and offered two illustrations for which a college president or a Board of Trustees would be at liberty to dismiss a faculty member, or otherwise restrict his right of expression. The first example was a professor who teaches that the world is flat and square. The other hypothetical case was a professor of history who might teach that secession was treason and that Robert E. Lee was a traitor. Hume said if an Ole Miss professor made such a claim, his chair of history should become "instantly vacant." And if the professor should claim that his academic freedom had been abridged, "The emphatic answer, coming quick and hot," would be, according to Chancellor Hume, "Sir,...you may not trample under foot what we regard as sacred as long as you hold a position in our institution."[23]

As *ex officio* chairman of the Board of Trustees, Governor Bilbo received Chancellor Hume's report but he was not swayed by it and shortly before the 1929 summer board meeting, he announced that he would again recommend that Chancellor Hume be replaced. The board again rejected Bilbo's recommendation and reelected Hume for another year. After this second setback Fred Sullens, in an editorial entitled "Forget It, Theodore," advised Bilbo to give it up. Sullens warned him that Hume's removal would provoke "bitter resentment among hundreds of 'Ole Miss' graduates, many of them prominent in public life…It would mean," Sullens said, "that these men will…throw every possible obstacle in the path of your administration."[24]

But Governor Bilbo would not abandon his goal of restructuring the governance of higher education or his effort to remove Chancellor Hume. In his third annual message to the legislature on January 6, 1930, Bilbo repeated his recommendations for a central Board of Trustees and a commissioner of higher education. He also requested a one million dollar bond issue for capital construction at Ole Miss. To those requests he added a rather startling addendum. Bilbo announced that he would recommend sweeping personnel changes, including faculty as well as presidents, at all of the state's institutions of higher learning in June. He had only two years left of his four year term, and at that point he had achieved virtually none of his major goals.[25]

Governor Bilbo was determined to improve Mississippi's institutions of higher learning and he would start at the top and work down. The *Jackson Daily News* reported the governor's annual message under the caption, "Bilbo promises Clean Sweep," and quoted the governor as saying that younger men were needed to lead the state's institutions of higher learning.[26]

Over the next few months, the subject of age and length of service figured prominently in any discussion of the impending shakeup at the state institutions of higher learning. It was frequently noted by the press that President Buz M. Walker of Mississippi A&M was approaching seventy years of age and that he had been associated with the college in one capacity or another for nearly fifty years. Robert E. Lee Sutherland, a former member of the Board of Trustees who was under consideration for president of MSCW, refused to tell reporters his age. "If it is necessary to say anything about my age," he told them, "you might say that I would pass for 48, perhaps younger." Sutherland was fifty-two at the time of his appointment as president of MSCW.[27]

Age and energy were not the only considerations in Bilbo's determination to bring new leadership to the state institutions, especially in Chancellor Hume's case. Bilbo had stated publicly several times that Chancellor Hume's educational philosophy was outmoded and that he did not have the vision to transform Ole Miss into the Greater University of Mississippi that he believed was essential for the state's economic and social development. Not only did he favor the removal of Hume, Governor Bilbo also wanted to increase the chancellor's salary from $4,800

Chapter 5 — The Bilbo Purge, 1928-1932

to $25,000, a whopping five hundred percent increase, which would enable the Board of Trustees to recruit an educator of national prominence.[28]

The board had rebuffed Bilbo in 1928 and 1929. In 1930, however, when he decided to extend his Purge to the faculty, he would operate from a much stronger advantage. Because of several additional appointments, Bilbo controlled a majority of the central board that governed the University, Mississippi A&M, MSCW, and Alcorn A&M. He did not control the board that governed Delta State Teachers College and his effort to replace President William Kethley was unsuccessful. He had already replaced the president of State Teachers College in Hattiesburg. Bilbo made no effort to replace Alcorn President Levi Rowen or reorganize the faculty.[29]

For several weeks before the June 1930 meeting of the central Board of Trustees, some MSCW alumni had lobbied for the appointment of Dean Nellie Keirn as president. She had been acting president since the death of President Fant in 1929. Dean Keirn "did not desire the presidency on a permanent basis" and advised the board that she preferred to remain as dean of the college. The alumni effort on behalf of Dean Keirn was linked to the broader effort to secure the appointment of a woman president. Even though MSCW was the first state-supported women's college in the country, it had never had a woman president. It was not until 1989, and after it had become coeducational, that Clyda Rent became MSCW's first woman president.[30]

The two candidates most seriously considered for the MSCW presidency were Claude Bennett, president of, and R. E. L. Sutherland, the former president of Hinds Junior College and a former member of the central College Board. After Bennett announced that he intended to stay at State Teachers College, the Board of Trustees elected Sutherland president of MSCW in 1930.[31]

Speculation over who would be appointed president of Mississippi A&M obscured the circumstances under which President Buz M. Walker was vacating that position. Walker was known as a Bilbo partisan and had helped raise funds for his 1927 campaign. Because of his alliance with Bilbo, the *Clarion-Ledger* assumed that Walker's position was safe and predicted that he would be reappointed. The assumption that President Walker would be reappointed because he was a Bilbo supporter is a telling point, and his subsequent removal is evidence that Bilbo's effort to reform higher education was not a punishment of his enemies or a political maneuver to reward his friends.[32]

President Walker had been the subject of widening criticism for several months before the June board meeting, and he was personally blamed by some alumni for the lack of growth at Mississippi A&M. Anticipating the worst, President Walker secured a position in North Carolina and announced his intention to leave Mississippi A&M at the end of his current contract in June. However, on the day of the board meeting, a group of A&M alumni met with the board and informed them that they had persuaded President Walker to reconsider, that he had done so, and that he wished to remain as president. That eleventh hour maneuver was not successful because Bilbo and the Board of Trustees had already decided not to reelect President Walker.[33]

There had been some speculation that Alfred Butts, a popular professor of education at the Agricultural College, might be elected president of either Mississippi A&M or Ole Miss. That possibility prompted some backroom maneuvering by Ole Miss alumni. They wanted to get Butts elected to the A&M position because they did not believe Bilbo had enough votes to dismiss Chancellor Hume and reinstate Joseph Powers. Their strategy was simple. By getting the A&M presidency for Butts would take him out of the running for the job at Ole Miss, and that would save Chancellor Hume. The Ole Miss faction was frustrated, however, because Butts was so complacent about either position that he was eventually eliminated from both. His elimination guaranteed that Hugh Critz would get the A&M presidency.[34]

Critz's appointment at A&M sealed the fate of Chancellor Hume. At the June board meeting, A.B. Schauber, a member of the Board of Trustees when Chancellor Powers was fired in 1924, nominated the former chancellor. Paul Bowdre, a Bilbo appointee, nominated Alfred Hume. Powers was elected by a vote of 6 to 4.[35]

It is probable that the shake up of the college presidents would have provoked no more than the customary gust of outrage, which would have soon faded. At the June meeting, and a later meeting on July 5, the Board of Trustees reorganized the faculty and staff at MSCW, Mississippi A&M, and the University. At Mississippi State College for Women ten faculty members out of a total of fifty-three were dismissed, and at least four staff members were not retained.[36]

At Mississippi A&M, in addition to President Walker, the director of extension and the director of experiment stations were also replaced. The Athletic Director was relieved of his duties, but retained as "Professor unassigned, outside of athletics, at the same salary." It is difficult to determine how many support personnel were fired or reassigned; there were slightly more than one hundred changes. That figure includes some home demonstration agents, county agents, experiment station workers, and clerical personnel and does not include faculty members. The best estimate of the number of faculty who were relieved or reassigned is twenty, certainly no more than twenty-five, out of a total of ninety-one. Exact figures are difficult to determine.[37]

The Purge at the University of Mississippi has been researched by Hardy Poindexter Graham, who found that it involved a relatively small number of professors and staff. The board minutes also contain much more information about the changes at Ole Miss than those at A&M and MSCW. On the same day that Joseph Powers was elected chancellor, Julius Zeller was elected vice-chancellor. Zeller was a state senator at the time of his appointment, and he listed farming as his occupation in the biographical section of the senate journal. The appointment of Senator Zeller is often cited as evidence that Governor Bilbo put hacks in high places because they were his friends, and that he took no accounting of their qualifications. Senator Zeller is the worst possible example. He had several college degrees, two from the University of Chicago, and a Doctor of Civil Law from Illinois Wesleyan University. He had also served as president of the University of Puget Sound. In 1930 the *Jackson Daily News* wrote that "there is not an abler member in either branch of the lawmaking body than Senator Zeller. He is both a scholar and a statesman." For several years, Zeller had been anti-Bilbo, but after failing to relocate the university, they joined in a common cause to enlarge and upgrade Ole Miss.[38]

Two weeks after Zeller's appointment, Chancellor Powers presented his faculty nominations to the Board of Trustees. The board declined to re-elect eighteen faculty members. The minutes of that meeting list the age and credentials of those eighteen faculty members, and in most cases include the credentials of their replacements. In every case, they were replaced by a professor with bona fide academic credentials equal to or superior to the individual being replaced. In most cases, the credentials of the new faculty members were superior. A good example is the dean of the graduate school. The graduate dean, who had been at the University for thirty-seven years, did not have a Ph. D. Governor Bilbo insisted that the dean of the graduate school be replaced by a younger man with a doctorate degree. The new graduate dean was Nathaniel Bond, who held a Ph. D from Tulane University.[39]

Most of the Ole Miss professors who were dismissed were in their late sixties or early seventies. Governor Bilbo recommended that faculty members in their mid-sixties, who were not retained, be given emeritus status with some compensation. But the legislature did not appropriate the necessary funds. Only a few of the faculty who were dismissed held graduate degrees, and several of them had only a bachelor's degree, which they had taken at the University of Mississippi. The unusually "large proportion" of faculty holding degrees from the University had been noted by the Southern Association of Colleges in 1929 and had brought an admonition to upgrade the University's faculty. Although most departments were affected by the Purge, Bilbo and the board did not disturb the history department chaired by Professor Charles Sydnor, who held a Ph. D and later enjoyed a distinguished career at Duke University.[40]

At least thirteen clerical and staff personnel were also replaced in addition to eighteen faculty members. One of those was the director of buildings and grounds. When he was informed of his dismissal, he fired off a letter to Governor Bilbo demanding an explanation: "Everyone in Lafayette County knows that I have championed your cause from your entry into Mississippi politics until the present time. So come clean...I want to know why." Several days later Governor Bilbo replied: "The chief cause of complaint seems to be that you were lazy or in other words, not as alert on the job as you might have been."[41]

One of the first and fiercest condemnations of the Purge came from Bilbo's old nemesis, Fred Sullens, who predicted that political intrusion into higher education would continue "until some clever brain devises a plan to remove our colleges wholly beyond the realm of political influence." He took no notice that Governor Bilbo had recently recommended such a plan to the state legislature.[42]

John Hudson, a free lance writer, described the Purge in a 1930 article, "The Spoils System Enters College," in *The New Republic*. Hudson reported that Bilbo had fired 50 professors at Ole Miss, 129 at other colleges and that 233 more were in jeopardy. Hudson's estimate of faculty members who were fired or in jeopardy totaled 412, when in fact there were only about 300 faculty members in the entire college system. According to Hardy Poindexter Graham, Hudson's article was an "extreme example of distortion and falsification."[43]

The best estimate of the Bilbo Purge includes three college presidents, eighteen faculty members at the University, ten at MSCW, and approximately twenty or twenty-five at Mississippi A&M. The number of staff and support personnel who were fired was no more than one hundred twenty-five. The reaction to the Purge was swift, severe, and subject to the most partisan interpretation. Lucie Robertson Bridgforth, in her 1984 history of the University of Mississippi School of Medicine, was among the earliest historians to offer a fair and balanced assessment of the Bilbo Purge. "In retrospect," she wrote, "there is little doubt that the University benefitted from the Bilbo changes in terms of personnel. There is also little doubt that Bilbo's intentions were honorable, for he clearly was determined to build a great university which would serve the state and all of its people, not just the privileged sons of the upper classes." Bridgforth also explains the complicated situation involving Dean Joseph Crider, who was fired but rehired, and then resigned. Historian Chester Morgan, in his biography of Governor Bilbo, also provides a more accurate appraisal of the Bilbo Purge and an explanation of how it has lingered as an historical inaccuracy for more than eighty years. "While some of the changes were patently political," Morgan explains, "there is ample evidence that the overall design was a sincere effort to improve higher education.... Although the extent of the dismissals, which included several Bilbo supporters, was greatly exaggerated, and that most of the replacements bore impeccable academic credentials, the almost universal enmity in the Mississippi press turned the whole affair into just another Bilbo scandal."[44]

Criticism from the opposition press was hardly more than a nuisance. But the loss of accreditation by educational associations was a repudiation of Bilbo's determination to modernize Mississippi's institutions of higher learning. The most serious damage to state institutions was the loss of accreditation by the Southern Association of Colleges and Schools. The Ole Miss law school was also expelled from the American Association of Law Schools and the medical school was placed on probation. But one medical association wrote to Chancellor Powers that "great good will no doubt come out of the whole mess.... Maybe the new dean can and will do what is needed...to build up the school." Two professional associations that conducted on site investigations did not censure the University. The American Pharmaceutical Association commended the new dean and allowed the school of pharmacy to retain its "A" rating. President Emeritus W. O. Thompson of The Ohio State University and the chairman of the American Association of State Universities' committee that investigated the Bilbo Purge, stated that John Hudson's *New Republic* article included many exaggerations and distortions. On the basis of Thompson's report, the Association of State Universities declined to censure the University of Mississippi and expressed its disagreement with the accrediting agencies that had done so. [45]

Some members of the Board of Trustees believed that the Southern Association's action was punitive and not entirely free of political taint. Whatever may have been the motive that caused SACS to suspend Mississippi's institutions of higher learning, Fred Sullens did not like it. Sullens wrote that the suspension was "cruel, wanton, brutal, unnecessary, and devoid of any semblance of constructive thought." Many Mississippians shared Sullens' anger at both the Southern Association and Governor Bilbo. And some saw it as an opportunity to "devise a plan to remove our colleges wholly beyond the realm of political influence," and they would cite the Bilbo Purge as proof that some dramatic reforms were necessary.[46]

Theodore Bilbo might have been "Governor Inglorious" as Wigfall Green called him, or "a slick little bastard" as William Alexander Percy described him. But for all the bad he did, he did some good, and he tried to do right, so the evidence suggests, in restructuring Mississippi's system of higher education. That is not to say that Bilbo was not guilty of wreaking revenge upon some of his enemies in higher education. It is to say that Bilbo tried to do what needed to be done. The Brookings Institution conducted a study of higher education in Mississippi a year after the Bilbo Purge and repeated with only slight modifications most of Bilbo's recommendations. As the Brookings study was being conducted, Mississippi was in the process of choosing a successor to Governor Bilbo, and its institutions of higher learning were again a prominent issue in the campaign.[47]

Chapter 5 Footnotes

1 *Jackson Daily News*, May 27, 1927; *Clarion-Ledger*, August 19, 1927.

2 Interview with Robert Farley May 15, 1979 at Oxford; Hardy Poindexter Graham, "Bilbo and the University of Mississippi, 1928-1932," (M. A. thesis, University of Mississippi, 1965), 14.

3 Thomas Turner Interview Oral History Collection, University of Southern Mississippi, Hattiesburg, Mississippi.

4 See T. Harry Williams, *Huey Long* (1969), Chapter 18, "I've Got a University," 491-526; for a study on the social and economic role of the American state university, see Norman Foerster, *The American State University, Its Relation to Democracy* (1937).

5 Graham, "Bilbo," 5, 12; on Bilbo's determination to restructure higher education and move the University of Mississippi to Jackson, see Larry T. Balsamo, "Theodore G. Bilbo and Mississippi Politics, 1877-1932" (Ph. D diss., University of Missouri, 1967) and Sansing, *University of Mississippi*, Chapter 9, "Bilbo and the Greater University," 215-247.

6 Cabaniss, *University of Mississippi*, 142; see also Charles Reagan Wilson, *Baptized in Blood: The Religion of the Lost Cause, 1865-1920* (1980).

7 Balsamo, "Bilbo," 163, 166; *Clarion-Ledger*, January 18, 1928.

8 McArthur, *Inaugural Addresses, 1890-1980*, 134-187; on the Greater University of Mississippi, see 146-147 and on restructuring higher education, see 152-153.

9 *Jackson Daily News*, January 19, 1928; see also Wigfall Green, *The Man Bilbo*, (1963) and Chester M. Morgan, *Redneck Liberal, Theodore G. Bilbo and the New Deal* (1985).

10 *Clarion-Ledger*, January 19, 20, 1928.

11 Cabaniss, *University of Mississippi*, 141-142; for a text of this and other speeches by Chancellor Hume, see Myra Hume Jones, "Tenets and Attitudes of an Old-Time Teacher," (M.A. thesis, University of Mississippi, 1949); for additional arguments against moving the University, see Friends of the University, *Some Facts Against Removal of the University of Mississippi* (n.d.).

12 *Oxford Eagle*, February 23, 1928, March 8, 1928; *Jackson Daily News*, February 15, 1928, March 7, 1928, September 18, 1928.

13 *Mississippian*, January 13, 1928.

14 Graham, "Bilbo," 3.

15 McLemore [ed.], *History of Mississippi*, II; see Chapter 39, "Higher Education in the Twentieth Century," 415-445; Graham, "Bilbo," 37-38.

16 *Mississippian*, April 6, 1928.

17 Cabaniss, *University of Mississippi*, 135. 141-143; Graham, "Bilbo," 32, 36.

18 Graham, "Bilbo," 32-33, 36-37.

19 William D. McCain interview at Hattiesburg, Mississippi on January 30, 1979; Graham, "Bilbo," 32-33; Francis Egger Watson, "Dr. Alfred Hume: His Leadership as Vice Chancellor, Acting Chancellor, and Chancellor of the University of Mississippi (1905-1945)," (Ph. D diss., University of Mississippi, 1987), 71-73.

20 Balsamo, "Bilbo," 210; *Hattiesburg American*, June 20, July 1, 1928; New Orleans *Times Picayune*,

May 31, 1928; *Jackson Daily News*, June 12, 1930; *Commercial Appeal*, June 2, 1930; *Jackson Daily News*, March 6, 1940; Willard F. Bond, *I Had a Friend*, (1958), 80-81; Alma Hickman, *Southern As I Saw It: Personal Remembrances of an Era, 1912 to 1954* (1966), 73, 84; Chester M. Morgan, *Dearly Bought Deeply Treasured: The University of Southern Mississippi 1912-1987* (Jackson, 1987), 45-52.

21 *Mississippian*, April, 27, September 28, 1929; Board of Trustees, *Biennial Report 1927-1929*, 14-21.

22 Graham, "Bilbo," 13-15; *Mississippian*, September 28, 1929; Sansing, *University of Mississippi*, 226-233.

23 Board of Trustees, *Biennial Report 1927-1929*, 14, 17.

24 *Jackson Daily News*, June 20, 1929.

25 *Senate Journal 1930*, 8-9.

26 *Jackson Daily News*, January 7, 1930; *Clarion-Ledger*, June 14, 1930.

27 John K. Bettersworth, *People's College*, 280; Balsamo, "Bilbo," 208; *Clarion-Ledger*, June 11, 14, July 6, 1930; *Jackson Daily News*, June 12, 1930; *Clarion-Ledger*, July 6, 1930; *Jackson Daily News*, June 15, 1930; *Commercial Appeal*, August 5, 1930.

28 Graham, "Bilbo," 15.

29 Bond, *I Had a Friend*, 141; *Clarion-Ledger*, June 12, 1930; Jack W. Gunn and Gladys C. Castle, *A Pictorial History of Delta State University* (1980), 27.

30 *Jackson Daily News*, June 11, 15, 1930; *Clarion-Ledger*, June 12, 15, 1930; Pieschel and Pieschel, *Loyal Daughters*, 88-90.

31 *Jackson Daily News*, June 11, 1930; *Minutes*, June 13, 1930.

32 *Clarion-Ledger*, June 5, 11, 1930; *Minutes*, June 13, 1930.

33 *Clarion-Ledger*, June 5, 11, 1930.

34 Ibid; *Jackson Daily News*, June 12, 1930.

35 *Minutes*, June 13, 1930; *Clarion-Ledger*, June 14, 1930.

36 *Minutes*, June 13, July 5, 1930; *Clarion-Ledger*, June 28, July 6, 1930; *Jackson Daily News* June 16, 1930; Pieschel and Pieschel, *Loyal Daughters*, 90-91.

37 *Minutes*, June 13, July 5, 1930; *Clarion-Ledger*, June 12, 28, July 3, 6, 1930; Ballard, *Maroon and White*, 44-46.

38 *Minutes*, June 13, 1930; Graham, "Bilbo," 40; *Jackson Daily News*, June 13, 1930; for a biographical sketch of Senator Zeller, see *Official and Statistical Register of the State of Mississippi, 1920-1924*, 135-140.

39 For a comparison of the credentials of the faculty dismissed and those who replaced them, see Graham, "Bilbo," 44-64.

40 Ibid.

41 These letters were in a folder marked "Higher Education" in the Theodore G. Bilbo Papers, William D. McCain Library, University of Southern Mississippi, Hattiesburg, Mississippi.

42 *Jackson Daily News*, June 15, 1930

43 John Hudson, "The Spoils System Enters College," *The New Republic* LXIV, (September 17, 1930), 123-124; see also Clarence Cason, "The Mississippi Imbroglio," *Virginia Quarterly Review* (April, 1931), 229-240; *Mississippi Educational Advance* (October 1930), 9 and also (November 1930), 41; Bettersworth, *People's College*, 208, relied on Hudson's figures and included this statement, "Before the 'terror' ended 112 members of the faculty at A&M had been dismissed and the positions of 233 others were in jeopardy;" Allen Cabaniss, *University of Mississippi*, was more careful in describing the Purge but he did not challenge Hudson's figures.

44 Lucie Robertson Bridgforth, *Medical Education in Mississippi: A History of the School of Medicine* (1984), 74; for a more recent history of the Medical School, see Janis Quinn, *Promises Kept, The University of Mississippi Medical School* (2005); and for an interesting reminiscence of the Medical School, see Robert D. Currier and Maurine Twiss, *Pressure From All Sides, The University of Mississippi Medical Center in the 60s* (2006); Morgan, *Redneck Liberal*, 45-46; see also Sansing, *University of Mississippi*, Chapter 9 "Bilbo and the Greater University, 1927-1935," 215-246.

45 Graham, "Bilbo," 78-79, 80-85, 91-94, 95-98, 98-99; see *Proceedings of the Thirty-fifth Annual Meeting of the Association of Colleges and Secondary Schools of the Southern States, Atlanta Georgia December 4-5, 1930*, 35-36.

46 *Jackson Daily News*, December 7, 1930

47 Green, *Bilbo*, 72; William Alexander Percy, *Lanterns on the Levee, Recollections of a Planter's Son* (1941), 148.

Chapter 6
A Constitutional Board of Trustees, 1932-1945

To attempt to keep politics out of [college] boards is just as vain as pursuit of a wraith across a meadow in the moonlight.

Senator David E. Crawley

During the 1931 campaign all of the candidates for governor, and several legislative candidates, promised the people of Mississippi that they would end the reign of politics at the state's colleges and pledged to the accrediting agencies that they would take politics out of the colleges, and take the colleges out of politics. For a variety of reasons, the voters found Martin Sennett Conner most convincing and elected him governor. Conner was a former Speaker of the House of Representatives and an implacable foe of Governor Theodore Bilbo.

One of the successful legislative candidates in the 1931 campaign was Joseph Anderson Cook, the former president of State Teachers College who was fired by Bilbo in 1928. Cook was elected to the state senate and soon after the legislature convened in January 1932 he introduced a lengthy, detailed measure designed by the wily old veteran of the school wars to place the institutions of higher learning "beyond the realm of political influence." Senator Cook's bill included some of the recommendations of the O'Shea and Brookings Studies. In 1930 the legislature commissioned the Brookings Institution to conduct a broad study that included Mississippi's educational system. The Brookings Institution recommended a nine member State Board of Higher Education with governing authority over the junior colleges and the institutions of higher learning. The nine trustees would serve nine year staggered terms. The Brookings Study also recommended the establishment of a Chancellor of the Greater University of Mississippi with authority over the junior and senior colleges to implement the "educational policies established by the proposed State Board."[1]

Senator Cook's bill, which was much less sweeping than the Brookings recommendation, passed with little opposition. The 1932 statute consolidated the three boards of trustees into one ten member board with governance over all six state institutions of higher learning, that included Ole Miss, Mississippi State, Alcorn A&M, MSCW, Mississippi Southern College at Hattiesburg, and Delta State at

Cleveland. Two trustees from each of the three supreme court districts, and three from the state at large, were appointed to twelve year staggered terms, with one third of the members rotating off the board every four years, and they could not succeed themselves. The tenth "trustee shall be a citizen of De Soto County [and] be known as the trustee for the LaBauve Fund, and serve for a term of four years." The LaBauve Fund was a tuition endowment for orphans from DeSoto County to attend the University of Mississippi. The LaBauve Trustee would only vote on issues that involved the University. The governor remained *ex officio* president of the board.[2]

According to the statute, to be eligible for membership on the new Board of Trustees "one must be a qualified elector of the supreme court district from which appointed, be at least twenty-five years of age, and must have won some recognition for moral and intellectual leadership in his community." The trustees were given the "power to make any adjustments they think necessary between the various departments and schools of any institution or between the different institutions."[3]

The statute did not establish a commissioner of higher education. Instead, it authorized the board to appoint an Executive Secretary and employ additional clerical staff the trustees deemed necessary. The Executive Secretary of the Board of Trustees was not given the authority that O'Shea or Bilbo or the Brookings Study had recommended for the commissioner of higher education. College presidents would not yield either their authority or their institution's autonomy to the new Executive Secretary, and his role was more administrative than executive. The 1932 statute also established a new funding procedure and college presidents were required to prepare detailed budgets estimating the expenditures at their institutions for the next biennium. A combined budget for all institutions would then be prepared by the Executive Secretary and submitted to the legislature thirty days prior to the opening of each session. The board was also required to submit a biennial report to the legislature accounting for the expenditure of public funds and detailing the condition of campus buildings, enrollment figures, and faculty workloads. On the basis of each institution's budget, and the board's biennial report, the legislature would make a single appropriation for higher education. That appropriation would go to the Board of Trustees, which in turn would allocate a portion of the total appropriation to each institution. Before the 1932 statute, the legislature made separate and individual appropriations directly to each institution.[4]

Two provisions of that law in particular were designed to protect the institutions of higher learning from political interference and to keep the institutions out of entangling political alliances. First, the statute gave college presidents the sole authority to nominate the faculty and staff at their institutions. And, although faculty tenure was not established, there was a general understanding that politics would not be a consideration in personnel matters, and that faculty members would be reappointed, in the words of the statute, "during the period of satisfactory service." It was the protection provided by that clause that Senator Cook, Governor Conner, and others hoped would at last end the reign of politics at the state's institutions of higher learning. The second provision prohibited college officials and influential alumni from lobbying the legislature in the interest of their favored institution. The law was specific in that regard: "No official, employee, or agent representing any of the separate institutions shall appear before the legislature or any committee thereof except upon the written order of the Board or upon the request of the legislature or a committee thereof."[5]

Following the enactment of this law, Governor Conner appointed ten new trustees whose first and most pressing duty was to regain the accreditation of Mississippi's institutions of higher learning. At its first meeting on March 1, 1932 the Board of Trustees appointed a committee to open negotiations with the Southern Association, and in July the board requested a formal review of the Mississippi situation. The board received a favorable response from the Association's Executive Secretary who advised the board to proceed with the reorganization of the state institutions.[6]

At its annual meeting in December 1932 the Southern Association restored provisional accreditation to Mississippi's institutions of higher learning and advised the Board of Trustees that all restrictions would be lifted when certain conditions were met. The Association required an increase in faculty salaries and an increase in general academic support funds. The Great Depression, however, precluded that possibility and even though salaries and support funds were not increased, in fact they were reduced, the Southern Association of Colleges, and other professional accrediting agencies, restored full accreditation over the next two years.[7]

One of the conditions that the Southern Association required for accreditation was the reinstatement of the administrators and faculty members who had been dismissed during the Bilbo Purge. To meet that condition the new Board of Trustees dismissed Chancellor Powers in June 1932 and reappointed Alfred Hume. That was the second time that Joseph Neely Powers had been dismissed as chancellor of the University of Mississippi. His double dismissal is unique in the history of higher education in Mississippi. MSCW President Robert E. Lee Sutherland was also fired in 1932 and replaced by Burney L. Parkinson. In April 1933 President Claude Bennett was dismissed at State Teachers College in Hattiesburg and replaced by Jennings B. George. The following July President Hugh Critz of Mississippi A&M, which was renamed Mississippi State College in 1932, was replaced by George

Duke Humphrey. Some faculty members and support personnel were also reinstated.[8]

In addition to the issue of accreditation and financial exigencies Mississippi's new consolidated Board of Trustees grappled with the problem of institutional autonomy. One of the board's priorities was to establish a role and scope for each institution, and as an initial step in that direction, the board abolished the engineering program at Ole Miss because it was an unnecessary and costly duplication of the engineering program at Mississippi State. Before venturing too far afield, the Board of Trustees retained the Division of Surveys and Field Studies at George Peabody College to study higher education in Mississippi and formulate a role and scope function for each of the state's six public institutions.[9]

At the time the Peabody Study was made Mississippi was supporting more institutions of higher learning per capita than any other southern state, and a larger percentage of its white students were in college than any other state in the region. According to the O'Shea Study, Mississippi's unusually high collegiate enrollment, especially for an impoverished rural state, was caused by the "eagerness" of white Mississippians "to have their children acquire a degree from a college or university, largely for the social value which it is presumed to possess." To capitalize on that "eagerness," and to garner their share of the student market, Mississippi's institutions of higher learning, according to one study, engaged in an "unseemly competition." More significant, they were forced to lower their admission standards and were induced to expand their course offerings and popular degree programs to attract greater numbers. These conditions made coordination increasingly difficult, but increasingly necessary.

A pressing need for statewide coordination was apparent to the Peabody Study team and they reiterated several recommendations made by O'Shea, Bilbo, and the Brookings Institution, in particular the assignment of specific missions to each institution and the establishment of a commissioner of higher education. The Peabody Study also cautioned the Board of Trustees against expanding graduate education and repeated the Brookings recommendation that the junior and senior colleges be consolidated into a single state system of higher education. The Peabody study team did not include Alcorn College in its survey and made practically no recommendations regarding higher education for blacks in Mississippi.[10]

Board members made a good faith response to the Peabody Survey's recommendations, but rather than establishing a single administrative officer for higher education the board created the Presidents Council, and directed the presidents to "stimulate thoughtful cooperation on the part of the colleges." Within two years after the Peabody Study was made the board advised the legislature that it had correlated the curriculum of each institution in accordance with its historical mission. The board listed the role and scope functions of the five white institutions as follows: [11]

> University of Mississippi: liberal arts, literature, humanities, social sciences, and professional schools resting essentially on the liberal arts; fine arts, law, medicine, pharmacy, economics, education, civil engineering, commerce, business, and graduate education.
>
> Mississippi State College: professional schools and departments resting essentially on the natural sciences; agriculture, engineering, mechanic arts, business and vocational education, graduate courses, and such general courses as are necessary to supplement its technical training.
>
> Mississippi State College for Women: a combination of undergraduate courses in fine arts, industrial arts, literature, languages, home economics, civics, social and natural sciences, teacher training, and courses suited for a well rounded cultural and practical education for girls.
>
> State Teachers College and Delta State Teachers College: professional courses for the training of teachers and allied subjects.

The board announced that it had followed "a safe course" in assigning exclusive functions to certain institutions. Courses or departments or schools, the board announced, would be eliminated only on the grounds of strict economy and then only after the long term needs of each institution had been fully considered. The board also authorized the Presidents Council and the Executive Secretary to study the feasibility of reactivating courses or departments that had been discontinued and the feasibility of adding new programs if there were a sufficient demand.[12]

That concession proved to be unfortunate because, as David Levine has found, "the free market had not proved efficient enough in education." Unlike the California Board of Regents, which created a single statewide system of colleges based on California's "genuine educational needs," Mississippi's Board of Trustees, in spite of the Peabody Study's admonition against it, sustained the tradition of institutional autonomy and invited college presidents and other clever academics to ply them with arguments for keeping old programs and for adding new ones. The lay Board of Trustees proved to be no match for the rhetoricians and mathematicians. Chancellor Hume calmly and convincingly cautioned the Board of Trustees against taking the Peabody Study too seriously. He told them to be especially wary of statistics which, "while having the appearance of reliable accuracy," are often misleading. That was especially true, Chancellor Hume continued, when dealing with "questions of education."[13]

The members of Mississippi's Board of Trustees deferred to the presidents of the colleges they governed on "questions of education," and Chancellor Hume persuaded the board to reestablish the school of engineering just four years after it had been abolished. President George Duke Humphrey of Mississippi State also persuaded the board to expand the school of business in spite of the fact that the Peabody Study had recommended its discontinuation. And in spite of the Peabody Study's specific recommendation against it, the board allowed Mississippi State to establish a graduate school in 1935.

There was general dissatisfaction, especially in the legislature, with the board's unsuccessful effort to coordinate the state colleges into a unified system. And the board's failure to reduce the duplication of degree programs prompted the introduction of bills in almost every legislative session during the 1930s to either consolidate or abolish some of the state institutions. In the 1934 session House Bills 344 and 345 were sponsored by thirty-five members of the house. Those bills would have abolished State Teachers College at Hattiesburg and Delta State Teachers College at Cleveland. Neither bill reached a vote on the house floor because they were withdrawn in favor of House Bill 555, which would have consolidated all of the state's institutions of higher learning into a university system. That bill was also defeated.[14]

In 1934 the rivalry among the white institutions of higher learning was so entrenched, and their supporters so territorial, that closing or consolidating any of the colleges was a political impossibility. In its effort to be fair, the Board of Trustees actually became indulgent, and allowed the institutions, including both teachers colleges and Alcorn A&M, to add new programs and expand existing ones without regard to the state's genuine educational needs.

If the new consolidated Board of Trustees gets low marks for its effort to coordinate the state's system of higher education, it probably deserves a failing grade for its effort to shield them from politics. There was evidence of that failure in the first general election following the board's establishment. The 1935 governor's campaign was a bitter contest between a millionaire businessman, Hugh Lawson White, and a "runt hog" populist, Paul Johnson, Sr. The campaign was acrimonious, even by Mississippi standards. In a one party system elections rarely turn on principles; they turn on personalities, and where there is no clash of political issues there is almost certain to be a collision of personal ambitions. In such a contest everyone is forced to take sides, and college officials and faculties lined up on one side or the other in 1935.

Chapter 6 — A Constitutional Board of Trustees, 1932-1945

In a press release issued shortly after his election Governor White accused several college officials and board members of playing politics during the 1935 campaign. Actually, his accusation was not so much that they took part in the election, but that they campaigned for the "other fellow." He specifically accused President Parkinson of MSCW, President George of the State Teachers College at Hattiesburg, John Lee Gainey, the business manager at the University of Mississippi, and William H. Smith, the Executive Secretary of the Board of Trustees. He also accused two board members of openly campaigning against him. After Governor White was inaugurated on January 21, 1936 rumors circulated that there would be several changes at the institutions of higher learning. It was also rumored that Governor White would recommend a reorganization of the Board of Trustees.[15]

At a press conference on February 18, 1936, Governor White announced his plans to reorganize the Board of Trustees. He waved a letter, and said if the people knew what was in that letter they would understand why he could not work with the existing Board of Trustees and why he needed a strong voice in the affairs of the state's educational institutions. Governor White declined to reveal the contents of the letter. He said that it was from a board member to a private citizen. The inference was that the letter was an appeal to support Paul Johnson, and Governor White implied that many other citizens had received similar letters. During the press conference Governor White also announced his intention to dismiss President Parkinson of MSCW.[16]

Several weeks prior to that press conference there were rumors that President Parkinson was in jeopardy, and MSCW students and alumni had written letters to the editor pleading with the governor not to dismiss him. Fred Sullens of the *Jackson Daily News*, who had endorsed Hugh White, responded to a letter from an MSCW student:

> Listen little lady, listen softly with both ears open. A few weeks hence there will be no parking place for President Parkinson on the campus at MSCW. In rude words it is this: President Parkinson is going to pass out. So are some other people.[17]

That cavalier commentary on the dismissal of President Parkinson is in stark contrast to Sullens' moral outrage at the Bilbo Purge five years earlier.

During his press conference Governor White also announced that he would ask the legislature to reorganize the Board of Trustees. He did not specifically endorse House Bill 242, which had recently been introduced. House Bill 242 would increase the number of board members from ten to thirteen. The three new members would serve four year terms and after their terms expired the number would revert to ten. The bill would allow Governor White to appoint seven new board members and that would give him control of the board. Governor White said that he did not particularly want a larger board, and if the trustees who had opposed him in 1935 would resign, he would be content to let the board remain at ten members.[18]

There was divided and diverse reaction to Governor White's intention to reorganize the Board of Trustees. The Columbus *Commercial Dispatch* recommended a reorganization of the entire state system of higher education and proposed the removal of four of the six college presidents. The *Dispatch* justified that radical proposal because some "members of the Board…used their office for political purposes."[19]

The *Commercial Dispatch* also accused the Board of Trustees of depositing large sums of money in certain banks. The editor concluded: "The colleges are under partisan political control. Therefore, Governor White ought to have the authority to add members to the Board." But the *Dispatch* reassured its readers that Governor White did not intend to inject politics into the affairs of the colleges. The governor only wanted a voice in the administration of the institutions for which he would be responsible. It was presumed, by that editor at least, that the governor was the head of the state's educational institutions.[20]

While the legislature was debating its options, a resolution calling for a reorganization and consolidation of the Mississippi system of higher education was introduced. Like several of its predecessors the bill got lost in the shuffle and never came to a vote. Hilton Waites, chairman of the house university and colleges committee, opposed the resolution consolidating the state institutions but supported House Bill 242 because he believed all state-supported institutions should be subject to the will of the people. During the debate on House Bill 242 Waites made derogatory remarks about the University and some Ole Miss students hanged him in effigy in early February 1936. A house resolution was hastily introduced and passed to "condemn the unseemly conduct" of the Ole Miss students. Theodore Smith, a young representative from Corinth, opposed the resolution on the grounds that the legislature had more pressing problems to address and should not waste its time reacting to college pranks.[21]

Some prominent legislators opposed House Bill 242 because they feared that any tampering with the College Board might be considered political interference by the Southern Association and might again jeopardize the accreditation of the state institutions. Walter Sillers introduced an amendment to the House Bill 242 that would prevent any person associated with an institution of higher learning from participating in politics "even to the extent of keeping them from voting." It is not clear if Sillers' amendment was an effort to kill House Bill 242, or if Sillers actually intended for his amendment to become law.²²

On the senate side of the capitol Joseph Cook, who had authored the 1932 bill establishing the consolidated board, reminded his colleagues that his bill had been designed to remove the colleges from politics. But, he was sorry to say, it had not done so and he favored increasing the number of trustees to give Governor White control of the board. Other senators supporting the house bill argued that the existing board had been permeated by politics from its beginning and that Governor White had promised to dismiss only those educational officials who had campaigned against him. In a rather strange logic, supporters of the bill advanced the theory that Governor White must fire several college officials as a means of keeping politics out of the institutions of higher learning.²³

Senator Frank Harper wanted to state for the record his reason for voting for the bill:

> I believe that the governor as the head of the affairs of the state ought to have full authority over the institutions of the state.... I voted to turn the affairs of the state over to Governor Conner and I am now voting to turn it over to Governor White.²⁴

House Bill 242 was passed on February 21, 1936, and the *Clarion-Ledger* reported its enactment in blazing headlines: CONTROL OF COLLEGES GOES TO WHITE. Although its passage boded ill for the state's institutions of higher learning, they did not suffer from any significant political intrusion during Governor White's administration. Neither President Parkinson, President George, nor the board's Executive Secretary was removed. But there was continuing support during Governor White's administration for consolidating some institutions of higher learning and for closing others. In 1937 Senator Bill Burgin introduced a bill to "disestablish" State Teachers College at Hattiesburg and make it the "Southern Branch of the University of Mississippi." The following year, Representative Joseph May of Simpson County introduced a bill to indefinitely suspend the operation of State Teachers College but neither bill passed. In 1940 the legislature enlarged and elevated State Teachers College to Mississippi Southern College.²⁵

College officials and board members apparently did not learn from their unhappy experience following the governor's election of 1935, and they were again involved in the 1939 campaign. After Paul Johnson, Sr. defeated former Governor Mike Conner, he announced that he would reorganize the Board of Trustees and remove one college president, and possibly more. Soon after Governor Johnson was inaugurated in January 1940, a bill was introduced to increase the Board of Trustees to fifteen members, which would give Johnson control of the board.²⁶

Both houses debated the bill extensively and in much the same spirit they had debated House Bill 242 four years earlier. Senator David Crawley of Attala County opposed the bill but admitted that any "attempt to keep politics out of [college] boards is just as vain as the pursuit of a wraith across a meadow in the moonlight." Senator James Rice of Natchez objected to "politicalizing" the board and the constant flux of its membership. Supporters of the bill argued that the increase in the size of the board was merely an extension of the courtesy they had accorded to past governors, and it was only fair to give Governor Johnson a majority on the board. The bill increasing the board to fifteen members was passed in early March, 1940.[27]

Fred Sullens, who had opposed Governor Johnson in 1935 and in 1939, reported the passage of the bill with a shout of "Hooray for ignorance!" and announced that "All persons who voted for him and are able to read and write should now apply for positions on the faculties of our institutions of higher learning." Those who could not read and write, he continued, might be employed if they can positively prove they had supported the governor.[28]

Shortly after Governor Johnson's new appointees joined the Board of Trustees, a new college was added to the number of institutions under the governance of that expanded board. On May 6, 1940, the legislature authorized the transfer of Jackson College to the state and changed its name to Mississippi Negro Training School. Mississippi's newest state institution of higher learning, was the second state college for blacks, and is now Jackson State University.[29]

The second reorganization of the Board of Trustees in a period of four years convinced many supporters of higher education that Mississippi's institutions of higher learning had not been removed from politics and argued that Governor Johnson had jeopardized their accreditation. Those fears were not unfounded and after his appointees took control of the Board of Trustees, Governor Johnson dismissed several administrators and faculty members at Mississippi Southern College.[30]

The Southern Association of Colleges reacted quickly. It placed Mississippi Southern College on probation, threatened to withdraw accreditation from the state's other institutions of higher learning, and warned the board that the Association would monitor the situation closely for any additional signs of political interference. The Southern Association's action rallied a small and dedicated group of men who were determined to find some way of shielding the institutions of higher learning from continued political intrusion.[31]

That small group of men included Oliver Emmerich, editor of the McComb *Enterprise*, and Circuit Court Judge John C. Stennis, a former member of the state legislature and future United States Senator. They met with Governor Johnson and discussed the possibility that Mississippi's institutions of higher learning might again lose their accreditation. As an alternative to the existing statutory board, they proposed a constitutional amendment creating a politically independent Board of Trustees. The advantage of a constitutional board, over a statutory board, would be that any change in its organization or modification of its authority would require a constitutional amendment, which is a much more complicated process than statutory revision.[32]

Early in the 1942 legislative session a constitutional amendment establishing a new Board of Trustees was introduced. With Governor Johnson's support it was passed by both houses in early March. The amendment was ratified during the general election in 1943 and became Article 8, Section 213A of the Mississippi Constitution. In the next legislative session a bill implementing the amendment was introduced and quickly passed. The law created a thirteen member Board of Trustees, appointed by the governor with the approval of the senate, to twelve year staggered terms with four members rotating off the board every four years. Twelve trustees were appointed from the seven congressional districts, the three supreme court districts, and two from the state at large. The thirteenth member was the LaBauve Trustee of DeSoto County, who served a four year term and legally could vote only on matters pertaining to the University.[33]

On March 30, 1944 Governor Thomas Bailey submitted his nominations for the College Board and they were confirmed by the senate. The new constitutional Board of Trustees met for the first time on May 18, 1944. It is ironic, given the great effort that went into the establishment of a politically independent board, that the *Jackson Daily News* heralded the new board's first meeting under the caption: FOOTBALL IS ASSURED FOR STATE COLLEGES. At its first meeting the board reinstated intercollegiate athletics, which had been cancelled in 1942 because of the war.[34]

The Board of Trustees was trying to get the colleges ready for the return of peace. With peace came the college boom, the dimensions of which few American colleges anticipated. Ignited by rising expectations, and sustained by the GI Bill, the postwar enrollment explosion changed the American collegiate system. The American college had been secularized after the Civil War. After World War II colleges were democratized. Perhaps the classic response to the democratization of higher education was the action taken by the New York Board of Regents. In the immediate aftermath of World War II the New York Regents established a statewide university system with the motto, "Let Each Become All He Is Capable Of Becoming."[35]

In postwar America, the college gates were opened wide.

Footnotes Chapter 6

1 *Laws 1932*, 383-388; see also Brookings Institution, *Report on a Survey of the Organization and Administration of State and County Government in Mississippi* (1932), Chapter 33, "Higher Education," 514-545.

2 *Laws 1932*, 383-388.

3 Ibid.

4 Ibid.

5 Ibid, 387.

6 Graham, "Bilbo", 107-118; *Minutes*, March 1, 1932; Bettersworth, *People's College*, 293-294.

7 *Proceedings of the Thirty-seventh Meeting of the Southern Association of Colleges and Secondary Schools at New Orleans, Louisiana,* December 1-2, 1932, 36.

8 Cabaniss, *University of Mississippi;* 148; Pieschel and Pieschel, *Loyal Daughters*, 94; McLemore [ed.], *History of Mississippi*, II, 432; Bettersworth, *People's College*, 313.

9 *Biennial Report 1934-1935*, 4.

10 See Frank P. Bachman, *Report of Functions of State Institutions of Higher Learning in Mississippi* (1933), cited hereafter as the *Peabody Study*, 1, 12-14; O'Shea Study, 200-205, 351; on socialization as a function of higher education, see Oscar and Mary Handlin, *The American College and American Culture* (1970).

11 *Biennial Report 1934-1935*, 6-7.

12 Ibid.

13 David O. Levine, *The American College and the Culture of Aspiration* (1986), 170-172; Jones, "Alfred Hume," 84-89.

14 *Mississippian*, February 17, 1932; *House Journal 1934*, 193-194, 270, 311.

15 *Jackson Daily News*, February 18, 21, 1936.

16 *Jackson Daily News*, February 18, 1936; *Clarion-Ledger*, February 21, 1936.

17 *Jackson Daily News,* February 18, 19, 1936.

18 Ibid., February 20, 1936; *House Journal 1936,*

19 Ibid., February 18, 1936, quoting the *Columbus Dispatch.*

20 Ibid.

21 *Jackson Daily News*, February 18, 20, 1936; *Mississippian*, March 7, 1936; University of Mississippi, Subject File, MDAH.

22 Ibid.

23 *Jackson Daily News*, February 21, 1936

24 *Senate Journal 1936*, 241.

25 *Laws 1936*, 322-326; *Clarion-Ledger*, February 21, 1936; copies of Burgin's and May's bills are in the University of Mississippi Subject File, MDAH.

26 McLemore, *History of Mississippi*, II, 435; *Hattiesburg American*, May 29, December 13, 1940; *Jackson Daily News*, March 7, August 1940; *Clarion-Ledger*, March 7, 1940.

27 *Jackson Daily News*, March 7, 1940.

28 Ibid., March 8, 1940.

29 *Biennial Report 1939-1941*, 53; see also Rhodes, *Jackson State University*, 25-27, 155.

Chapter 6 — A Constitutional Board of Trustees, 1932-1945

30 McLemore [ed.], *History of Mississippi*, II, 435.

31 Ibid.; see also *Proceedings of the Thirty-seventh Meeting of the Southern Association of Colleges and Schools, 1940*, 156-157.

32 Interview with Senator John C. Stennis at Starkville, Mississippi on May 30, 1979; see the John C. Stennis Collection at Mitchell Memorial Library, Mississippi State University, for letters, documents, and clippings concerning the establishment of the constitutional Board of Trustees; for a recent biography of Senator Stennis, see Don H. Thompson, *Stennis: Plowing a Straight Furrow* (2015).

33 *Jackson Daily News*, February 27, 1942; *Laws 1942*, 438-439; *Laws 1944*, 454-469.

34 *Jackson Daily News*, May 19, 1944; the *Clarion-Ledger* cut line read: "New College Board to Resume Football Schedules."

35 For the impact of World War II on American colleges, see Rudolph, *American College*, 483-487.

Chapter 7
Governing the College Boom, 1945-1962

I took a small college and made it a big university.
President William D. McCain
University of Southern Mississippi

After all the talk about taking politics out of the colleges, politics intruded upon the first meeting of the new constitutional Board of Trustees. For several weeks prior to the board meeting on May 18, 1944, there were rumors that a professor at Delta State Teachers College and the Executive Secretary of the Board of Trustees would be fired. Theodore Bilbo, who was then a United States Senator, had accused the Delta State professor of openly espousing racial equality. J. A. Ellard, the Executive Secretary, was also supposed to be fired because he had campaigned for Governor Thomas L. Bailey's opponent in the 1943 campaign.[1]

Although the charges against the Delta State professor were not brought before the board, and his fate was not discussed, a motion was made to fire the Executive Secretary. Oliver Emmerich, a McComb newspaperman who had been instrumental in creating the constitutional board, introduced an amendment to the motion to fire Ellard. Emmerich's proviso stipulated that if the motion to fire Ellard passed it would carry with it his resignation because "I've worked too hard and too long to get a constitutional Board." Emmerich added that the Secretary had "served under a political Board and he had to cater accordingly [but if] he would show any signs of playing politics next week or the week after, I'd be willing to fire him."[2]

Emmerich's assertion was convincing and the motion to dismiss Ellard was withdrawn. That unheralded incident was a turning point in the history of higher education in Mississippi and marks the transition of the College Board from a political instrument to a public institution. That made it possible for Chancellor J. D. Williams to fend off an effort by Governor Fielding Wright to have a certain person appointed to a position at the university. Shortly after his appointment in 1946, Chancellor Williams received a telephone call from Governor Wright "instructing him to appoint a certain person head of the university laundry." The next day Chancellor Williams drove to Jackson to discuss the matter with the governor. Governor Wright told the chancellor that during the telephone conversation he had a state senator in his office. The governor then explained to Chancellor Williams, who had only recently come to Mississippi, "You have your row to hoe, and I have mine." The meeting ended amicably and Chancellor Williams did not make the appointment.[3]

It was fortunate for Mississippi's collegiate officials that they were not distracted by petty politics because they were soon consumed by an enrollment explosion. On August 20, 1945, Acting President Clarence Dorman of Mississippi State College wrote to the Board of Trustees expressing his great relief that the war was over, and predicted that the GI Bill would make it possible for "thousands" of veterans to go to college who "would not have attended college under ordinary circumstances." He then repeated Chancellor John Waddel's commitment to the veterans when the University reopened after the Civil War. President Dorman said, "we cannot turn them away."[4]

The postwar enrollment explosion revived the debate over the role of higher education in American society, and it was evident that the role of the college and university was changing. Some resisted that change and others encouraged it; almost everyone discussed and studied it. Perhaps the most influential study of higher education was President Harry Truman's Commission on Higher Education, which concluded that "American colleges and universities must…no longer consider themselves merely the instrument for producing an intellectual elite." Higher education, according to the President's Commission, must encourage Americans to form a new world view in recognition of the "oneness of the modern world."[5]

World War II was the war that changed everything.

In the end it was not the commissions or faculties or governing boards that determined the character of high education in postwar America. The students "took charge of change" and by their sheer numbers redefined the American college and university. In 1870 1.7% of the college age Americans were in college; in 1900 4.01% were in college; by 1948 20% were in college. A collegiate curriculum designed for less than two percent or even four percent could not meet the demands of twenty percent and colleges began adding new courses. The old curriculum was abandoned, and collegiate education was defined by student demand.

Higher education in Mississippi experienced a similar enrollment pattern. In 1900 college enrollment in Mississippi was 2,727, with 2% of the college age population in college. By 1950 the student enrollment increased to 21,716, with almost fifteen percent of the college age group enrolled; by 1960, college enrollment was 35,473.[6]

The last year of the war enrollment at Mississippi State College was 761. In the first full academic year after the war enrollment was 3,391; almost 75%, or 2,458, were veterans. At Ole Miss during the spring semester of 1945, enrollment was 657. In the fall semester, enrollment was 1,271. A year later enrollment reached 3,213.

Chapter 7 — Governing the College Boom, 1945-1962

In the fall of 1944 enrollment at the former State Teachers College in Hattiesburg, which was renamed Mississippi Southern College in 1940, was 264. In 1946 it was 1,189. At Jackson College for Negro Teachers the 1944 enrollment was 195. In 1946 enrollment was 633 and over 500 veterans were turned away. President Jacob Reddix told the Board of Trustees that Jackson College, if it had the facilities, could enroll 1,000 students during the regular academic session and over 2,500 in the summer session. Delta State Teachers College had 205 students in 1945 and 891 three years later. Alcorn and Mississippi State College for Women experienced less dramatic gains largely because of Alcorn's remoteness and because dormitory facilities at MSCW limited enrollment to approximately 1,250. Mississippi's private colleges experienced similar though less dramatic enrollment growth.[7]

As Mississippi entered the postwar college boom the College Board realized that it must act quickly if expansion was to be controlled and directed. To provide a data base for some quick and difficult decisions the board retained Joseph E. Gibson to conduct a general study of higher education in Mississippi and asked W. T. Sanger to survey the state's need for medical education.[8]

While Gibson and Sanger were conducting their studies, the board was trying to govern the institutions of higher learning under circumstances that were less than ideal. Several college presidents were embroiled in public controversies and agitated alumni groups were calling for new leadership. The board realized that the changing role of higher education would require a new philosophy of governance, and the board replaced four college presidents during its first two years.

The first president to be dismissed was William H. Bell of Alcorn, who "leaned altogether towards arts and sciences" rather than vocational training. President Bell was replaced by William H. Pipes who was committed to making Alcorn an agricultural college in the best land grant tradition. President Pipes told the Board of Trustees that to fulfill its mission Alcorn must either be moved to a more central location, or it must be made accessible by hard surface roads. President Pipes' determination to upgrade Alcorn was frustrated by the fact that the board assigned Jackson College the role of providing general education courses for Mississippi's burgeoning black college enrollment.[9]

At its next meeting the board dismissed Mississippi Southern College President Jennings B. George, who "stood like a rock against loose living" and was "horrified to discover that faculty members and students did their shopping uptown on Saturday afternoon." He believed it was undignified for scholars to shop on "the day that was reserved for the common people to shop." After spurning the board's request to resign, President George was dismissed. Six months later President George Duke Humphrey of Mississippi State failed to win a vote of confidence and resigned. At its next meeting the Board of Trustees voted not to re-elect Ole Miss Chancellor Alfred Butts because, "it was best for the university." When President Burney L. Parkinson of MSCW could not be persuaded to resign, the board passed an automatic retirement policy that forced his retirement.[10]

Joseph E. Gibson published his study of higher education in the early fall of 1946 and chastised the board for not having implemented more of O'Shea's recommendations. Gibson stated bluntly that the Board of Trustees must design a role and scope for each of Mississippi's institutions, and see that they remain within the parameters of that design. Gibson warned the College Board, "the price of allocation of functions is eternal vigilance."[11]

Before getting down to the nuts and bolts of role and scope, Gibson flirted with a pipe dream. He wondered about the wisdom of consolidating all of the state's white institutions of higher learning into one Greater University of Mississippi at Jackson. Gibson acknowledged that consolidation was not popular, but he said the study committee "felt compelled" to recommend this "excellent way of achieving most of the things the Board and the people of Mississippi so earnestly desire." Gibson asked rhetorically, "What greater monument could the first constitutional board bequeath its state than this greater University of Mississippi?"[12]

Because the college boom would reshape all of Mississippi's institutions of higher learning, Gibson assessed the needs of black higher education at some length and concluded that those needs were not being met. Consequently, Gibson recommended a new vocational school for blacks to be located somewhere in the Delta. Acting on that recommendation, the legislature established Mississippi Vocational College at Itta Bena, which opened in 1950 with an enrollment of 300. Gibson did not recommend that Alcorn be closed, although he did question the wisdom of maintaining Alcorn in its remote location and suggested that the board at least consider merging Alcorn with Jackson College.[13]

The Board of Trustees did not implement most of Gibson's recommendations, and the board actually did one thing the study recommended that it not do. W. T. Sanger, who made the study of medical education, recommended that the board maintain the two year medical school at Oxford rather than establish a four year program at Jackson. However, the Board of Trustees organized a new medical center with a full complement of medical degrees and health related graduate programs, and in 1950 the legislature created the University of Mississippi Medical Center in Jackson.[14]

Largely on the basis of the Gibson Study the board assigned role and scope functions to each institution and accepted the assurances of college presidents that they would thoughtfully expand their degree programs with a minimum of duplication. Mississippi's institutions of higher learning were overwhelmed in the early postwar years, and curriculum expansion was dictated by student demand not board policy. College enrollment zoomed from four thousand in 1920 to ten thousand in 1940, to twenty thousand in 1950, to thirty-five thousand in 1960, to fifty-five thousand in 1965 and to seventy thousand in 1970. As the board was assigning role and scope functions to each institution, circumstances would eventually force the board to abandon those assignments and would alter the traditional hierarchy, or "pecking order," of higher education in Mississippi.[15]

The appointment of President Fred Tom Mitchell at Mississippi State in 1945 joined "the time and the man." To the delight of State's faculty, students and alumni, President Mitchell promised that he would not rest until Mississippi State is "literally the academic equal of its peers." He disdained the "academic penury" that Mississippi State's historical mission had imposed on it and directed his faculty to design a curriculum that would meet Mississippi's "ever changing demands." As enrollment soared from 761 in 1945 to 4,000 in 1949, the temptation to design a curriculum by student demand was too tempting to resist. During the college boom President Mitchell created a new image for the institution and brought a new sense of self esteem to Mississippi State alumni.[16]

In many ways the expansion at Mississippi State College for Women best illustrates the college boom in Mississippi and symbolizes the interaction between the college campus and the society that sustains it. Shortly after the war MSCW officials abandoned school uniforms and permitted students to keep automobiles on the campus. With the uniforms went the traditional role of women in Mississippi society, and with the cars came an upward mobility. The route to its record enrollment was a curriculum that offered students what they wanted. In rapid succession MSCW added five new degree programs, and in one year alone fifty-five new courses were added. Most of those new courses were in liberal arts and business and other academic areas not traditionally associated with women's colleges. Mississippi State College for Women, though it had denied for fifty years that it had any intention of doing so, seemed to be "invading the sphere of men."[17]

When Robert C. Cook became president of Mississippi Southern College in 1945, it was a small college located in the state's most rapidly growing section. Its alumni had long envisioned Mississippi Southern as a liberal arts college, and maybe even a university some day. To the hearty approval of its faculty and students and alumni, President Cook pledged to expand the curriculum at Mississippi Southern and prophesied that its enrollment would "skyrocket." His prediction came true sooner than he expected. During the first three years of his administration enrollment quadrupled, with over half of those students in liberal arts and business

95

courses. Southern billed itself as the "Cinderella" of Mississippi's institutions of higher learning.

President Cook had been a member of the faculty at the University of Mississippi before the war and he understood the traditional roles of the state's institutions of higher learning. The 1932 consolidated Board of Trustees, with the tacit approval of the state's political and educational leadership, had established a priority pyramid with the University as the "capstone of public education" in Mississippi. Mississippi State came next, then Mississippi State College for Women, then Mississippi Southern and Delta State, and finally Alcorn. That "pecking order," was never voiced by the state's public officials and certainly not by members of the Board of Trustees; it was, however, a reality that President Cook and other college presidents had lived with before the war.[18]

Chancellor John D. Williams realized that enrollment growth and curriculum expansion at Mississippi's other white institutions would undermined the traditional role of the University "as the capstone" of higher education in Mississippi. As the Board of Trustees, the legislature and the general public attached increasing importance to enrollment figures, Ole Miss officials found themselves arguing that "the size of the on campus student body is by no means an adequate basis for judging the expense of operating an institution of higher learning." The original missions, and the traditional roles of institutions of higher learning, according to Chancellor Williams, "are the most reliable standards" for the allocation of state funds.[19]

During the college boom the faculty and friends and alumni of the other white institutions of higher learning decided that it was not the University of Mississippi's prerogative to be "the capstone," and they considered their institutions peers, not subordinates, of the state university.

One of the most important dimensions of the postwar college boom in Mississippi was the transformation of higher education for African Americans. The College Board soon realized that its long tradition of "making haste slowly" was no longer an option.

To blacks in postwar Mississippi higher education was the avenue of upward mobility, the "yellow brick road" to the American dream. Few white Mississippians understood the hold that dream had on blacks, and their determination to reach it. One of those who did was Hodding Carter, the Pulitzer Prize winning editor of the *Delta Democrat Times*, who delivered the commencement address at Alcorn College in 1948. When asked to summarize his speech Carter explained,

> I felt that what I said to them was not needed, for I had advised them not to be content with the manifold inequalities

experienced by their race.... I know that they are identical in their aspirations and their good citizenship with college graduates anywhere [and] there can be no good reason for fearing or longer subjugating any American who dreams our common, sturdy dream of a fair chance and a place, our place, in the sun. That's all those Alcorn graduates want, and it's the least that they deserve."[20]

Most board members realized that higher educational opportunities for blacks, even after the establishment of Mississippi Vocational College at Itta Bena in 1950, were unequal to those for whites. In the hope of postponing that day when black students would seek "the same opportunities" available to whites, the board established a scholarship program that paid the tuition, and in some cases other expenses, for blacks who went out of state to obtain graduate and professional degrees that were not available at Mississippi's black institutions.

The College Board was reluctant to establish new graduate and professional programs at the black institutions. Nevertheless, the college boom forced the board to restructure the curriculum at Jackson College. In 1940 the enrollment at Jackson College was 131. In 1949 2,500 students enrolled in its summer session and hundreds more were turned away. In the midst of the college boom the Board of Trustees issued a new mission statement for the state's three black institutions of higher learning. Alcorn would continue to offer teacher training and home economics and would emphasize mechanical arts, agriculture, and allied sciences. Mississippi Vocational College would also offer some teacher education, but stress vocational training. Under its new mission statement Jackson College was significantly expanded. Jackson College would become a liberal arts college offering a broad range of undergraduate degrees in the arts and sciences, and graduate degrees in a few selected fields.[21]

Almost immediately after World War II black veterans began to challenge Mississippi's Closed Society, and there was an "undercurrent of nervous apprehension," as there had been just after the Civil War, that some aggressive black student might seek admission to one of the state's white institutions of higher learning. To prevent the integration of Mississippi's colleges and universities, in August 1950 the Board of Trustees empowered college presidents to "accept or reject any applicants according to the best interest of everyone."[22]

Three years after the board adopted that policy, Charles Dubra, who had a bachelor's degree from Claflin College and a master's degree from Boston University, met with Robert Farley, dean of the Ole Miss law school. Dubra explained that he would like to be admitted to the law school but did not want any publicity connected with his admission. He said he was not an activist and would live quietly off campus in the Oxford black community.

Dean Farley and Chancellor Williams met with the Board of Trustees and recommended that Dubra be admitted. The board president favored his admission, but one board member "got almost violent over the idea." The trustees rejected Dubra's application on the grounds that Claflin College was unaccredited, even though his graduate work at Boston University would have made him eligible for admission. Dubra accepted the board's decision and did not seek legal redress.[23]

In the summer after Dubra's rejection, the United States Supreme Court issued the *Brown* decision, and Medgar Evers, a graduate of Alcorn A&M, applied for admission to the Ole Miss law school. Although the Board of Trustees made no public disclosure of his application, a Jackson newspaper reported that Evers had applied to the law school and had been rejected. Rather than pursue his application to Ole Miss, Evers accepted a position with the NAACP.[24]

The militant phase of the civil rights movement began in Mississippi, as it did elsewhere, on the college campus in the springtime.

In May 1958 Clennon King, a controversial professor at Alcorn A&M who had been dismissed the year before, appeared at the Lyceum in Oxford and informed the registrar that he wanted to apply for a Ph. D in history, which the University did not offer at that time. When he was left alone for several minutes in an office in the Lyceum, he opened a window and began shouting "Help! They are going to kill me!" Professor King was taken into custody by the Highway Patrol, and a judge sent him to Whitfield for a mental examination. He was released a few days later and left the state.[25]

In stark contrast to the Clennon King fiasco at Ole Miss, Clyde Kennard made formal application for admission to Mississippi Southern College in September 1959.

The Clyde Kennard story is a dark and sorry episode in Mississippi history.

Clyde Kennard was a Korean War veteran who owned a small poultry farm near Hattiesburg. After he submitted an application to Mississippi Southern College in September 1959, the Forrest County Cooperative foreclosed on his poultry farm and confiscated his stock. The Southern Farm Bureau canceled his automobile insurance, and the State Sovereignty Commission tried to get his bank records, but the local bank refused its request. On September 25, 1960 Johnny Roberts, a nineteen year old black man, stole twenty-five dollars worth of chicken feed from the Forrest County Cooperative and sold it to Kennard. On the basis of Roberts' testimony, that Kennard knew it was stolen, Clyde Kennard was arrested, convicted by an all white jury, which deliberated ten minutes, and was sentenced to seven

Chapter 7 — Governing the College Boom, 1945-1962

years in Parchman prison.

While he was serving his sentence at Parchman, Kennard developed intestinal cancer. State officials did not want the unfavorable publicity of Kennard dying in Mississippi jailhouse, and gave him an early release. Kennard was rushed to Chicago for emergency surgery. He was beyond recovery, and died on July 4, 1963.

On December 31, 2005 *Clarion-Ledger* reporter Jerry Mitchell interviewed Johnny Roberts who admitted that his testimony against Kennard was false, and that he had been pressured by local officials to implicate Kennard. Following that article, there was a groundswell of support for the exoneration of Clyde Kennard. The University of Southern Mississippi had already begun that process in 1993 by naming its student services building for both Clyde Kennard and Dr. Walter Washington, a former student at USM and President of Alcorn State University. On May 17, 2006 Circuit Judge Bob Helfrich threw out the 1960 conviction of Clyde Kennard.[26]

One of the most remarkable aspects of the Clyde Kennard episode is that his name, which appeared in newspaper headlines, in the secret files of the State Sovereignty Commission, in legal documents of both state and federal courts, and in the records of Parchman prison, did not appear in the minutes of the Board of Trustees of State Institutions of Higher Learning. Members of the board who served during those troubled years, when interviewed two decades later, could not recall his name ever being brought before them or ever making any decision concerning his application. There was such need for unanimity and conformity in Mississippi's Closed Society that the College Board and college officials deferred to the state's power structure on matters that threatened the "Mississippi Way of Life."

While the state's power structure was dealing with race and rights and riots, Chancellor Williams was trying to convince the College Board that Mississippi could not support more than one comprehensive university. He stripped the issue of role and scope of its academic folderol and asked the board in October 1959, "Shall Mississippi develop one great university recognized nationally and regionally," or shall we have two universities or three universities "of lesser stature?" Chancellor Williams added, "I do not recommend combining any of the present institutions; my proposal is to allocate further appropriations for highly specialized doctoral programs to one specific place." In stating the obvious Chancellor Williams concluded, "It is too expensive and impractical for the state to permit duplication by institutions in these areas."[27]

However obvious or wise Chancellor Williams' proposal may have been, it had come too late. Mississippi State College had already been given university status and the legislature had already expanded the mission of Mississippi Southern

College. It would also become a university within a decade. Delta State Teachers College had been renamed Delta State College in 1955 and its curriculum, course offerings and degree programs were expanded. In 1956 Jackson College for Negro Teachers was renamed Jackson State College and both its graduate and undergraduate divisions were enlarged. Two decades later Mississippi would be supporting not one, not two, not three, but eight universities.

Although the board may have preferred to devote its attention to academic issues, and role and scope, the election of Governor Ross Barnett in 1959 signaled a return of politics to the board's deliberations and decisions. In less than a year after his appointees joined the board there was evidence that Governor Barnett and his counselors would become deeply involved in academic and even student affairs.

In the spring of 1961 Bill Barton ran for editor of the *Mississippian*, the Ole Miss student newspaper. Barton had worked as an intern for the *Atlanta Constitution* and had covered the sit-in demonstrations in Atlanta during the summer of 1960. On the basis of information supplied by the Georgia Bureau of Investigation, the Mississippi State Sovereignty Commission had mistakenly identified Barton as a participant in those demonstrations and had compiled a dossier on him. He was officially classified in the Sovereignty Commission files as an "agitator." While Barton was campaigning for editor in the spring of 1961, the Sovereignty Commission, with Governor Barnett's approval, leaked that erroneous information and Barton was defeated. Governor Barnett's acquiescence in the Sovereignty Commission's effort to influence a student election was but a prologue to his involvement in the James Meredith Crisis.[28]

Footnotes Chapter 7

1 Interview with President Emeritus William D. McCain, Hattiesburg, Mississippi, on January 30, 1979; J. Oliver Emmerich Interview, Oral History Collection, University of Southern Mississippi, Hattiesburg, Mississippi; for the impact of World War II on Mississippi see Neil McMillan, [ed.], *Remaking Dixie, The Impact of World War II on the South* (1997).

2 Ibid., see also J. Oliver Emmerich, *Two Faces of Janus, The Saga of Deep South Change* (1973).

3 James C. Read, "The Williams Chancellorship at the University of Mississippi, 1946-1968," (Ph. D diss., University of Mississippi, 1978), 158.

4 Board of Trustees, *Biennial Report*, 27, 29.

5 President's Commission on Higher Education, *Higher Education for American Democracy* (1947) 6 vols; for President Harry Truman's letter of appointment see *Establishing the Goals*, I, v.

6 McLemore [ed.], *History of Mississippi*, II, 438-439.

7 *Biennial Report* 1943-1945, 47; *Biennial Report* 1945-1947, 8-9, 21, 26, 33, 36, 40, 44; *Biennial Report* 1947-1949, 2; Bettersworth, *People's University*, 307; Cabaniss, *University of Mississippi*, 159-160.

8 *Minutes*, August 23, 1944.

Chapter 7 — Governing the College Boom, 1945-1962

9 Dunham, *Alcorn College*, see Chapter X, "The Administration of William H. Bell," 59-63 and Chapter XII, "The Administration of Dr. William H. Pipes," 67-71.

10 *Jackson Daily News*, January 26, 1945; *Clarion-Ledger*, June 15, 45; Hickman, *Southern As I Saw It*, 115-116; interview with Reece D. McLendon, September 21, 1981, Senatobia Mississippi; McLendon was a member of the Board of Trustees in 1945, a former student of President George's, and personally delivered the board's request that President George resign, and after he refused to resign, McLendon moved that he be dismissed; Pieschel and Pieschel, *Loyal Daughters*, 106; *Minutes*, January 24-31, 1952; *Jackson Daily News*, January 24, 1952.

11 Joseph E. Gibson, *Mississippi Study of Higher Education* (1945), 31-33, 38.

12 Ibid, 46-48.

13 Ibid, 332-333, 337; see J. H. White, *Up From the Cotton Patch, J. H. White and the Development of Mississippi Valley State College* (1979) and Sammy Jay Tinsley, "A History of Mississippi Valley State College," (Ph. D diss., University of Mississippi, 1972).

14 See *Gibson Study*, Chapter XI for the study's recommendation concerning medical education, specifically see 151-166; see also Bridgforth, *Medical Education in Mississippi* (1984), 104-105.

15 John E. Brewton, *Higher Education in Mississippi* (1954), 278-279; for enrollment growth see McLemore [ed.], *History of Mississippi* II, *439; Commercial Appeal*, July 22, 1948.

16 *Biennial Report 1947-1949*, 20-21; Bettersworth, *People's University*, 304-306.

17 Pieschel and Pieschel, *Loyal Daughters*, 107, 111-117, 119-121.

18 Robert Cecil Cook Interview, Oral History Collection, University of Southern Mississippi; *Minutes*, March 16, 1948; Hickman, *Southern as I Saw It*, 121.

19 *Biennial Report 1947-1949*, 10; *Biennial Report 1949-1951*, 18. 31.

20 For a summary of Carter's address see Dunham, *Alcorn A&M College*, 70-71; for biographies of Carter see James E. Robinson, *Hodding Carter: Southern Liberal, 1907-1971* (1974) and Ann Waldron, *Hodding Carter, The Reconstruction of a Racist* (1993).

21 *Minutes*, January 18, 1951; *Biennial Report 1949-1951*, 7; Tinsley, "Mississippi Valley," 63-64; Rhodes, *Jackson State University*, 116-120.

22 *Minutes*, August 15, 1950.

23 Interview with Dean Robert J. Farley, Oxford, Mississippi, May 15, 1979; Russell Barrett, *Integration of Ole Miss* (1965), 25.

24 Mrs. Medgar Evers, *For Us, The Living* (1967), 114-119; *Minutes*, September 16, December 16, 1954; for a recent biography of Medgar Evers see Michael Vinson Williams, *Medgar Evers: Mississippi Martyr* (2011).

25 Interview with Judge James P. Coleman, June 16-17, 1979, Oxford, Mississippi.

26 Interview with President Emeritus William D. McCain; Zack J. Van Landingham, "Report on Clyde Kennard to the State Sovereignty Commission;" this dossier was compiled by the Sovereignty Commission and was found in Governor Barnett's papers in the MDAH, and a copy is in the Holmes Collection; see also Ronald Hollander, "One Mississippi Negro Who Didn't Go To College," *The Reporter* (November 8, 1962), XXVII, 30-34; for a letter to the editor from Clyde Kennard, see *Hattiesburg American*, December 6, 1958; see also Timothy J. Minchin and John A. Salmond, "The Saddest Story of the Whole Movement: The Clyde Kennard Case and the Search for Racial Reconciliation in Mississippi, 1955-2007," *JMH* vol. 71, 191-234.

27 *Biennial Report, 1947-1949*, 10; *Biennial Report 1951-1951*, 18.

28 Read, "Williams Chancellorship," 174.

Chapter 8
The Meredith Crisis, 1962-1963

*I returned to my home state to replace the old unsuitable
customs with more desirable ones.*

James Howard Meredith

The admission of James Howard Meredith to the University of Mississippi was a crucial event in the Civil Rights Movement and a turning point in the history of Mississippi. In the summer of 1962, Chancellor John D. Williams was asking the alumni to help him protect freedom of speech at Ole Miss, in the fall he would be asking them to help him save the University.[1]

Meredith's application triggered a mechanism that had been in place since 1954. A copy of his application and other correspondence was sent to the Executive Secretary of the Board of Trustees and six copies were sent to the state Attorney General. The number of copies sent to the Attorney General was later reduced because University officials were concerned that some copies might fall into the wrong hands.[2]

Mississippi's white power structure, in consort with the Board of Trustees, employed a strategy of delay in the hope of dissuading Meredith from his bid to break the color barrier in Mississippi. Their strategy was based in part on their experience with Charles Dubra and Clennon King, but mainly on the hope that Meredith might just go away if they did not let him in. Before he filed his application, Meredith wrote the NAACP Legal Defense Fund requesting legal assistance in the event a costly court case was necessary to gain admission. After receiving Meredith's application, the registrar informed him that the deadline for applications had expired and advised him not to appear for registration.[3]

After that initial rejection Meredith informed the justice department of his application to the University of Mississippi. His letter reveals the anguish that he and "his people" experienced in a Closed Society:

> Whenever I attempt to reason logically about this matter, it grieves me keenly to realize that a...citizen of a free, democratic nation, has to clamor with such procedures...to gain just a small amount of his civil and human rights.[4]

James Meredith was seeking the rights that Hodding Carter had told those

Alcorn graduates in 1948 were "the least that they deserve."

Until Meredith received the letter of rejection, he had maintained a low profile, and University authorities and state officials maintained strict secrecy. But after his official rejection, James Meredith filed a class action law suit on May 31, 1961 in the federal district court. His NAACP attorney, Mrs. Constance Baker Motley, wanted to appeal directly to the College Board. Meredith preferred a suit because he believed the courts would decide the issue swiftly and painlessly.

Federal District Judge Sidney Mize found and ruled that University officials "gave no consideration whatsoever to the race or the color of the plaintiff." Judge Mize further ruled that the admission policies adopted by the Board of Trustees, even those enacted after Meredith filed his application, were not designed "in any attempt direct or indirect, to discriminate against anyone solely on the grounds of race and color." Judge Mize concluded: "The testimony shows, and I find as a fact, that there was no discrimination against any student…solely because of his race or color."[5]

Meredith appealed Judge Mize's ruling to the Fifth Circuit Court in New Orleans. Circuit Judge John Minor Wisdom was baffled by the hearing in the district court that he said had been argued "in the eerie atmosphere of never-never land." The Circuit Court ordered a trial on Meredith's request for a permanent injunction.[6]

After a sometimes bizarre trial, Judge Sidney Mize ruled on February 3, 1962 that Meredith was not denied admission because of his race.[7]

Meredith appealed Judge Mize's ruling, and on June 25, the Fifth Circuit reversed the district court and directed Judge Mize to order Meredith's admission. "In every other state but Mississippi, that would have solved the matter," according to Ole Miss Professor Russell Barrett. "Instead," he said, "it soon became clear that he had reached but one more detour of the many that remained."[8]

As incredulous as Judge Mize's initial ruling was, the Board of Trustees adopted a policy that was even more incredulous. The trustees divested the University of its authority over "the application of James Howard Meredith" and vested that authority "exclusively unto this Board of Trustees of Institutions of Higher Learning." A week later, on September 10, 1962, United States Supreme Court Justice Hugo Black ordered the admission of James Meredith, and on September 13, Judge Mize directed the University of Mississippi to admit Meredith.[9]

On the evening of Judge Mize's order to admit Meredith, Governor Ross Barnett addressed the people of Mississippi on a statewide television network. He said that Mississippi had only one of two choices: "We must either submit to the unlawful dictates of the federal government, or stand like men and tell them NEVER!"

Governor Barnett pledged to go to jail if necessary and called upon all other public officials to make a similar commitment, and he promised that no school would be integrated as long as he was governor. Under a 1954 constitutional amendment, Governor Barnett had the authority to close any or all of the state's public schools to prevent integration and his oblique reference to that authority startled many Ole Miss alumni who feared that Barnett's counselors might persuade him to close Ole Miss. Within a few days after Barnett's speech, a secret committee of Ole Miss alumni was organized with the singular purpose of keeping the University open, even if it meant admitting Meredith.[10]

The day after Governor Barnett's televised address, the Board of Trustees held a called meeting in Jackson. The discombobulation of the board began at that three hour "stormy" session on Friday, September 14. During the weekend, while board members were anxiously awaiting an explanation of his strategy to prevent Meredith's admission, Governor Barnett began a series of telephone conversation with President John Kennedy, Attorney General Robert Kennedy, and other officials at the Justice Department.[11]

Bill Minor's memoir, *Eyes on Mississippi, A Fifty Year Chronicle of Change*, which includes his articles that were published in the New Orleans *Times Picayune* from September 16, 1962 to May 19, 1963, provides a fascinating contemporary account of the Meredith Crisis.

On Monday, September 17, board members returned to Jackson for a closed meeting with Governor Barnett, who discussed the options in their legal battle with James Meredith. Governor Barnett mentioned two other possibilities that shocked the board members. First, he raised the possibility of closing the University. Then, he asked the board if they would be willing to accept contempt citations and go to jail. After Governor Barnett left the meeting, the trustees held a lively discussion.[12]

After that stormy meeting, a reporter asked several trustees if the University was going to be closed. The board president explained that the trustees did not have the authority to do so, but the governor did. The intimation that the University could be closed, subtle though as it was, sounded an alarm. The Ole Miss alumni realized that the University was in jeopardy, and there were some, even in high places, who would sacrifice the University of Mississippi for the cause of white supremacy and segregation. Although board members had agreed not to make any public statements, Verner Holmes thought that "was a great mistake" and decided that "somebody from the board should say something." As he was leaving the September 17 meeting, a reporter asked him if he was willing to go to jail. Holmes, an Ole Miss alumnus and vice-president of the board, declared: "I am not willing to go to jail [and] I will not vote to close the University."[13]

As tension and speculation mounted, and as the date of Meredith's registration neared, a Hinds County justice of the peace issued an injunction setting aside the United States Supreme Court order to admit James Meredith to the University of Mississippi. Editor Ira Harkey wrote, "In a madhouses's din, Mississippi waits. God help Mississippi." Harkey was the Pulitzer Prize winning editor of the *Pascagoula Chronicle*, and one of the few editors who criticized Governor Barnett's policy of defiance.[14]

While Mississippi was waiting, the board met in a midnight secret session to give Governor Barnett one last chance to convince them that he had a legal way "to keep him out." Verner Holmes remembered that five hour meeting at the Medical Center "as the worst experience of the whole thing." After hours of a rambling discussion, a frustrated trustee shouted to the governor: "We've got to know what is the legal way to keep him out, that's all we want to know." The governor's exasperated reply shocked his supporters and confirmed the worst suspicions of his detractors: "The only way I know to keep him out is just don't let him in." When it became apparent that "He actually had no plan, no way of doing it," tempers began to flare, and angry words and threats were exchanged.

During that frantic session, the board found an alternative to compliance or contempt. On September 4, the board had assumed the authority to act on the application of James Meredith to shield Chancellor Williams and other University officials. If the board had the power to divest the University of Mississippi of its authority to register Meredith, the board had the power, they reasoned, to confer that authority upon the Governor of Mississippi. At that midnight meeting at the Medical Center, the board designated Governor Barnett registrar of the University of Mississippi. That stratagem had been considered among Barnett's advisers. It was brought before the board inadvertently when a trustee said to the governor Barnett in frustration, "We'll let you do it. We'll let you reject him." That strategy was soon implemented.[15]

On Thursday afternoon, September 20, 1962, James Meredith and a small escort of federal officials arrived on the Ole Miss campus and were led through a noisy but not unruly crowd of students to a small auditorium where Governor Barnett and Registrar Robert Ellis were seated at a table. Following an exchange of friendly greetings, according to folklore, Governor Barnett asked, "Which of you gentlemen is Mr. Meredith?" Meredith identified himself and Governor Barnett then read a Declaration of Interposition, which, he claimed, allowed him to interpose himself as governor between an unlawful dictate of the federal government and the execution of that dictate in the sovereign state of Mississippi. Then, on the basis of the authority vested in him by the Board of Trustees as registrar of the

University of Mississippi, Governor Barnett denied James Meredith admission to the University of Mississippi. Following another brief but polite exchange Meredith and his escort left the campus and returned to Memphis.[16]

Because James Meredith had now been officially denied admission, a three judge panel in Hattiesburg issued a contempt citation against the Board of Trustees and ordered the board to appear in New Orleans on September 24 to show cause why they should not be held in contempt. University officials were also ordered to appear with the board in New Orleans.[17]

The news that the board had been cited for contempt raised the anxiety level among Governor Barnett's counselors. Some of them had already advised the governor to vacate the existing board and appoint a more stalwart group. On Saturday, the day after the board had been ordered to New Orleans, Governor Barnett huddled with his advisors at the Governor's Mansion for a strategy session. "It was the day of the Mississippi State-LSU game," is how one board member remembered the day of that meeting. The meeting was attended by fifteen or twenty of Barnett's advisors, including the Executive Secretary of the Citizens' Council. There was no focus to the meeting and a wide ranging, freewheeling review of circumstances and possible options were discussed. The only agreement among the various constituencies represented at the meeting was that compliance or capitulation were "unthinkable."[18]

On Sunday afternoon, the day after that strategy session in the Governor's Mansion, a different kind of meeting was held in Jackson. William Mounger, president of Lamar Life Insurance Company; Baxter Wilson, an executive in the Mississippi Power and Light Company; Tom Hederman, publisher of *Jackson Daily News-The Clarion-Ledger;* and Calvin Wells, chief counsel for Lamar Life, met in Wilson's office to discuss the general state of affairs. They were convinced that Mississippi's business leadership should do something, and they agreed to talk with their colleagues and get back together as soon as possible.[19]

On Monday morning, September 24 in federal court in New Orleans, Board President Thomas Tubb informed the court that the board had unanimously voted to register Meredith at 2:00 o'clock the next day in Jackson. The board was polled in the court room and each member present voted yes. The one absent member was polled by telephone and he also agreed.[20]

Realizing that the board's decision would excite the public, William Mounger and Calvin Wells directed the management of WLBT and WJDX, which were owned by Lamar Life, to "tone down" their editorials. At a meeting at the Medical Center Monday night, Mounger, Wilson, and Wells were joined by Ed Brunini, Bob Herrin, Joe Latham, and one or two other Jackson businessmen. They all agreed that the College Board had no other choice. But they were concerned about the repercussions and agreed to call other businessmen across the state and invite them to a private meeting in Jackson to discuss the crisis, which they feared could lead to massive violence. They also agreed to meet again the next night.[21]

On Monday night, September 24, Attorney General Robert Kennedy called Governor Barnett to arrange for Meredith's registration the next day. Governor Barnett was so upset by the board's decision that he could not carry on a coherent conversation with Kennedy and frequently interrupted their talk to confer with his advisors. The governor finally ended the conversation: "I am in a big hurry here now. I appreciate your calling. I will let you know tomorrow whether or not I can advise you of our proceeding and…" Attorney General Kennedy interrupted, "And work out his protection?" Barnett answered, "I will let you know what our proceedings will be."[22]

On Tuesday morning as board members were returning to Jackson from their New Orleans court appearance, a large crowd gathered at the Woolfolk building and Governor Barnett and his emissaries occupied the board office. When President Tubb learned that the board office had been commandeered, he instructed Executive Secretary Jobe to tell the board members to meet him in the restaurant at the Sun-N-Sand, a motel across the street from the Woolfolk building. Back on Mississippi soil, under threat of imprisonment, meeting in a motel coffee shop, and with two members absent, the Board of Trustees reaffirmed its unanimous vote to admit James Meredith to the University of Mississippi.[23]

When Executive Secretary Jobe got to his office, he found Governor Barnett sitting at his desk, talking to Robert Kennedy, who had just informed him that Meredith was on his way to the Woolfolk building to register. When Chief United States Marshal James McShane and James Meredith arrived at the Woolfolk building, they were led through a milling crowd of two thousand to the boardroom. A Barnett aide rapped sharply on the closed door, the governor appeared, and again asked, this time for the television cameras, "Which of you gentlemen is Mr. Meredith?" After Meredith identified himself, the governor again read a proclamation denying him admission to the university, and added that he did so politely. The federal officials, mocking the governor, agreed to leave politely. As they walked down the corridor Governor Barnett called out, in a practiced afterword, "You'll come see me at the Mansion." He turned back into the crowded boardroom amid cheers and Rebel yells.[24]

James Howard Meredith is a remarkable man. He marches to the sound of a different drummer, he made history, and he recognized history when he saw it. As Meredith and his federal escort were leaving the Woolfolk building their car stopped at a traffic light, and he saw history happening on a street corner, as he recalled in his memoirs:

> Just as the light was about to change, Marshal McShane asked me if those were some of my friends, indicating a group of six or seven Negroes standing on the corner. I waved at them as we pulled away.... They were all common folk, my people, maids still in uniform and common laborers, but...the pride they displayed [was] overwhelming. This is what I was fighting for, and I had my reward in the brief seconds that I saw my unknown friends on that corner.[25]

Early the next morning in search of some resolution, Assistant Attorney General Burke Marshall called Tom Watkins, one of Governor Barnett's most trusted advisors, who suggested that on the next effort to escort Meredith onto the campus to be registered, federal officials should "gently" push the Governor aside, but they should use "the mildest kind of force." Watkins explained that this would make the Governor's point, and give him an out because the federal government would have forcibly brought about desegregation. That pantomime was put to a quick test.

When Meredith and his escort arrived at the campus on Wednesday morning September 26, they were blocked by Lieutenant Governor Paul Johnson and several highway patrolmen. When John Doar of the Justice Department and Marshal McShane attempted to "gently" push their way through, Lieutenant Governor Johnson, Jr., jostled with McShane and Doar. After a few minutes, McShane doubled up his fist, shook it in the face of Lieutenant Governor Johnson, and said, or perhaps he was asking, "You understand that we have got to break through." Apparently Johnson did not understand or was not let in on the deal or, more likely, he did not want to be remembered as the "one who stepped aside." When all the fist shaking and shoving was over, Doar, McShane, and Meredith left Oxford and returned to Memphis. And the telephones started ringing.

When Marshall called Watkins and asked him what went wrong, Watkins told him that he "had not used enough force." How much force is enough force, Marshall asked? Watkins suggested that the next escort should include "twenty-five marshals with side arms." Marshall agreed to bring Meredith back to the campus the next day, Thursday, September 27, with an escort of twenty-five armed marshals "if it were clearly understood that the resistance to this amount of force would be token." Watkins said he would talk to the governor and get back with him.[26]

Over the next several hours, a bizarre haggle ensued. It was first agreed that the lead marshal would draw his gun, but Governor Barnett later decided that was not enough show of force. It was then agreed that the lead marshal would draw his gun, and that the other marshals would slap their holsters as if ready to draw. That was acceptable, at first, but Governor Barnett began to have second thoughts and he told the Attorney General:

> General, I was under the impression that they were all going to draw their guns. This could be very embarrassing. We got a big crowd here and if one pulls his gun and we all turn it would be very embarrassing. Isn't it possible to have them all pull their guns?[27]

As this haggling continued, Robert Kennedy pressed the governor for a guarantee that he would keep the peace and protect Meredith and the marshals. When Barnett wavered, Kennedy called the whole deal off and directed McShane and Doar not to take Meredith to the campus Thursday afternoon.[28]

After this impasse developed, President Kennedy decided to call Governor Barnett on Saturday morning to join the search for a peaceful resolution of the Meredith Crisis. The affable young president from Massachusetts and the wily old governor of Mississippi had a pleasant talk. President Kennedy assured the governor that he would use all the resources of his office to carry out the court order. The governor explained to the president that his aide Tom Watkins was at that very moment trying to work out a plan to resolve the situation.[29]

Within less than an hour, the president and the governor were back on the telephone. The president called Barnett back to discuss a proposal Tom Watkins had just made to the Attorney General. President Kennedy put Robert Kennedy on the line to explain the plan. Watkins had suggested a "hidden ball trick." The plan was for federal authorities to announce that Meredith would go to the campus on Monday, October 1. On the basis of that information, Governor Barnett and Lieutenant Governor Johnson would both be at Oxford to block his admission. In the meantime Meredith would go to Jackson where he would be registered in the board office. Governor Barnett could claim that the Kennedys had misled him. President Kennedy even agreed to let Barnett scold him in the sternest language if that would serve his political interest. With Meredith registered, Barnett would declare the battle was lost and would allow Meredith to attend the University of Mississippi. Governor Barnett was enthusiastic about the proposal as a solution to the impasse.[30]

While President Kennedy and Governor Barnett were working out the details of the "hidden ball trick," about one hundred businessmen and women were meeting secretly in Jackson on Saturday morning. They had come to that clandestine meeting in response to telegrams and calls from Mounger, Brunini and the small group of Jackson businessmen who had met several times over the last week or ten days. They represented the power structure in Mississippi, but they had waited too long to influence the course of history and prevent a violent confrontation between federal and state authorities.³¹

Throughout Saturday afternoon and into the early evening, Governor Barnett tried to persuade his counselors to accept the agreement he had made with the president. By game time, Barnett had lost his own resolve to honor it. At the Ole Miss-Kentucky football game that night in Jackson Governor Barnett was called to speak at half time. As the governor was speaking the world's largest rebel flag was unfurled to the stirring strains of "Dixie." The stands were awash in a sea of rebel flags. On that haunting night, those flags were more than a symbol of college spirit; they were a political statement.

Known fondly as Ole Ross, Governor Barnett was one of Mississippi's last great stump speakers. In his raspy, throaty voice, his right fist clinched, rising and falling, circling in rhythm with the words, Ole Ross proclaimed from the fifty yard line:

> I love Mississippi…
> I love her people…
> I love her customs…³²

Governor Barnett's half time speech was thrilling to many, and puzzling to some. After the game former governor J. P. Coleman talked briefly with former Governor Hugh White as they were leaving the stadium. Governor White said, "J. P. do you know what's going on about this Meredith business?" Coleman replied that he did not know what the situation was at that point. Governor White surprised Coleman by saying, "I don't understand Ross making that speech because I know that he has already agreed to admit Meredith."³³

After the game, Governor Barnett called the justice department. His call was forwarded to Attorney General Kennedy who had gone home. Governor Barnett told Robert Kennedy that he wanted to call off the deal. Kennedy was angered by that unexpected turn of events, and accused the governor of breaking his word to the president. The two men ended the conversation amicably with Barnett agreeing to keep working on the situation. Governor Barnett also promised to call Kennedy early Sunday morning to let him know if the situation changed through the night. President Kennedy was called at the White House and told that the deal was off. He reluctantly signed the documents federalizing the Mississippi National Guard, and authorized Secretary of the Army Cyrus Vance to send troops to Oxford and the University if it became necessary.³⁴

On Sunday morning, September 30, 1962, Governor Barnett called Attorney General Kennedy. That disjointed conversation dragged on for thirty minutes and Governor Barnett made one last desperate effort to postpone the whole affair. Failing at postponement, Governor Barnett proposed another mock confrontation between federal and state authorities. His suggestion was fraught with calamitous potential. Robert Kennedy rejected it, and threatened to reveal the secret tapes that had been made of their conversations.

Governor Barnett was startled to learn that his conversations with federal authorities had been taped and that President Kennedy might reveal those negotiations on national television unless a solution was found to the impending crisis. Bobby Kennedy realized that he had finally gotten through to the governor and he took advantage of Barnett's fear of exposure. Tom Watkins and Burke Marshall then worked out a plan to bring Meredith to the campus later that afternoon. Unfortunately, and unbelievably, university officials were not notified that Meredith and a federal escort were on the way to the campus.[35]

Through the late afternoon and early evening, a milling crowd of students gathered in front of the Lyceum, which had been cordoned off by federal marshals. Meredith was in his dormitory room in Baxter Hall and would register in the Lyceum the next morning. The crowd was gradually augmented by "outsiders" and by night fall, the crowd was much larger and more restive. At 7:30 p.m., Governor Barnett announced on a statewide radio and television network that Meredith was on the campus. He explained that he had been forced to yield to the "armed forces and oppressive power" of the United States and that he had conceded to Meredith's admission to prevent violence and bloodshed.[36]

At approximately eight o'clock, just moments before President Kennedy went on national television to announce that Meredith was safely on the campus and would register the next morning, the crowd surged toward the marshals and the order to fire the tear gas was given. As the marshals fired the gas into the surging mob several people, including some highway patrolmen, were hit by the canisters and suffered fractures and broken bones. The pep rally atmosphere was gone and most of the college kids, who had just come to see what was happening, went with it. Only the real resisters, the true believers, remained to fight what Willie Morris has called the "Echoes of a Civil War's Last Battle." Two men were killed on that tragic night. Hugh Clegg, Chancellor Williams' executive assistant, blamed the riot on the "trigger happy" federal marshals who "jumped the gun."[37]

Early on Monday morning, October 1, 1962, James Meredith went to the Lyceum, registered, and paid his fees. He then hurried off to an eight o'clock history class. Before James Meredith was enrolled at Ole Miss no other public school in Mississippi, not a grammar school, high school, or college, had been integrated. Public parks, playgrounds, libraries, beaches, theaters, doctor's offices, lunch counters, cafes, water fountains, hospitals, hotels, motels, cemeteries, everything in Mississippi was segregated. James Meredith graduated from the University of

Chapter 8 — The Meredith Crisis, 1962-1963

Mississippi in August 1963.

The color barrier was broken, and there was a crack in the Closed Society.

Footnotes, Chapter 8

1 For a chronology of the legal steps leading to Meredith's admission, see Barrett, *Integration at Ole Miss*, Appendix A, 247-251; for Meredith's discussion of his admission, see *Three Years in Mississippi*, (1966) and James Meredith, with James Doyle, *A Mission From God, A Memoir and Challenge for America* (2012); see also Walter Lord, *The Past That Would Not Die* (1966); James W. Silver, *Mississippi: The Closed Society* (1966); Nadine Cohodas, *The Band Played Dixie, Race and the Liberal Conscience at Ole Miss* (1997); William Doyle, *An American Insurrection, James Meredith and the Battle of Oxford, Mississippi 1962* (2003); Henry T. Gallagher, *James Meredith and the Ole Miss Riot: A Soldier's Story* (2012); Meredith Coleman McGee, *James Meredith: Warrior and the America That Created Him* (2013); for the definitive study of James Meredith and Ole Miss, see Charles Eagles, *The Price of Defiance, James Meredith and the Integration of Ole Miss* (2009); see also Eagles, *Price of Defiance,* 20-21, for the intriguing story of Harry S. Murphy, Jr., a black student who attended Ole Miss under the Navy V-12 program in 1945; see also Stanford History Professor Allyson Hobbs, *Special to CNN*, February 5, 2014, "The 'White' Student Who Integrated Ole Miss;" Professor Hobbs' book on Murphy is expected to be published in 2015.

2 Hugh Clegg, "Someone Jumped the Gun," Unpublished Manuscript, Special Collections John D. Williams Library, University of Mississippi; for a recent biography of Clegg, see Ronald F. Borne, *Troutmouth, The Two Careers of Hugh Clegg* (2015).

3 Meredith, *Three Years in Mississippi*, 58.

4 Ibid., 59.

5 Ibid., 105ff; *Meredith vs. Fair, Transcript of Record*, II, 217, 220.

6 *Meredith vs. Fair*, II, 228, 232, 238-239, 241-243.

7 See *Transcript of Record*, III, for the testimony and the court's ruling; see also Jack Bass, *Unlikely Heroes*, (1981), Chapter 9, "Crisis in Mississippi," 172-201.

8 See *Transcript of Record*, V, 734, 737-739; Bass, *Unlikely Heroes*, 180-181; Barrett, *Integration at Ole Miss*, 82.

9 *Minutes*, September 4, 1962; Barrett, *Integration at Ole Miss*, 249.

10 For a complete text of Governor Barnett's speech, see the *Clarion Ledger*, September 14, 1963; interview with Charles Fair, Chairman of the Board of Trustees, September 18, 1978, Louisville, Mississippi; *Jackson Daily News-The Clarion Ledger*, September 16, 1962; see also Clegg, "Jumped the Gun" for the names of an alumni steering committee that he said "saved" the University; see also David G. Sansing, "Standing Guard, 150 Years of The University of Mississippi Alumni Association," *Ole Miss Alumni Review* (Fall 2002), 36-50.

11 *Minutes*, September 14, 1962.

12 For the positions of various board members, see transcripts of interviews in the Holmes Collection; also Verner Smith Holmes-Euclid R. Jobe Interviews; a copy of the Transcripts of the Barnett-Kennedy telephone conversations is in the Holmes Collection.

13 *Jackson Daily News*, September 18, 19, 1962. *Washington Post*, September 20, 1962.

14 *Pascagoula Chronicle*, September 19, 1962; see also Ira Harkey, *...dedicated to the proposition ... Editorials from The Chronicle* (1963) and *The Smell of Burning Crosses* (1967); Carl Wiesenburg, *The Oxford Disaster... The Price of Defiance* (1962); Weisenburg, a member of the state legislature from Jackson County, and Joe Wroton of Greenville, were the only two state legislators who publicly opposed Barnett's policy of defiance.

15 See Interviews with Tubb, Fair, Evans, Riddell, Stone and Holmes-Jobe in the Holmes Collection.

16 Barrett, *Integration at Ole Miss*, 107-108.

17 *Jackson Daily News*, September 21, 1962, New Orleans *Times Picayune*, September 22, 1962; Barrett, *Integration at Ole Miss,* 109; Lord, *The Past That Would Not Die*, 157.

18 Interview with S. R. Evans, a member of the Board of Trustees, on October 13, 1978.

19 Interview with William H. Mounger on September 21 and 28, 1978 at Jackson Mississippi.

20 Interview with Thomas J. Tubb on September 18, 1978 at West Point, Mississippi.

21 Mounger Interview.

22 Transcripts of the Barnett-Kennedy Tapes, September 24, 1962; Verner S. Holmes and Euclid R. Jobe Interviews. 23; Tubb Interview.

24 Tubb interview; *Jackson Daily News*, September 26, 1962; *Times Picayune*, September 26, 1962; see also Robert Canzoneri, "*I Do so Politely: A Voice from the South* (1965).

25 Meredith, *Three Years in Mississippi*, 196.

26 Transcripts of the Barnett-Kennedy Tapes, September 26, 1962; *Daily Mississippian*, September 27, 1962; Meredith, *Three Years in Mississippi*, 202-203; Transcripts of the Barnett-Kennedy Tapes, September 27, 1962.

27 Transcripts of the Barnett-Kennedy Tapes, September 26 and 27, 1962.

28 Ibid.

29 This conversation is not included in the Transcripts of the Barnett-Kennedy Tapes, but excerpts from this conversation, from which the above quotation is taken, may be found in Hugh Clegg, "Jumped the Gun," 179-181.

30 Ibid.

31 Mounger Interview; copies of those telegrams are in the Holmes Collection.

32 *Jackson Daily News-The Clarion Ledger*, September 30, 1962; interview with Gerald Blessey, July 22, 1975, by Hank Holmes, in Mississippi Department of Archives and History, Jackson, Mississippi.

33 Holmes-Coleman Interview.

34 George B. Leonard, T. George Harris, and Christopher S. Wren, "How a Secret Deal Prevented a Massacre at Ole Miss," *Look* (December 31, 1982), 22 ff.

35 Transcripts of the Barnett-Kennedy Tapes, September 30, 1962.

36 Barrett, *Integration at Ole Miss*, 146.

37 Willie Morris, "At Ole Miss: Echoes of a Civil War's Last Battle," *Time* (October 4, 1982), 8-11; see Eagles, *The Price of Defiance*, Chapter 18, "The Riot," 340-370.

Chapter 9
Higher Education in Troubled Times, 1963-1972

We are in troubled times.
President M. M. Roberts, Board of Trustees

While James Meredith was studying for his final exams in the summer of 1963, Mississippi was in the midst of an election that fundamentally changed Mississippi politics. It was the last "lily white" election, and the first election since Reconstruction in which a Republican was a serious candidate for governor. Lieutenant Governor Paul Johnson defeated Rubel Phillips, the Republican candidate, in the November general election.

In the fall campaign, Rubel Phillips published transcripts of the telephone conversations between Ross Barnett, Paul Johnson, and the Kennedys that revealed for the first time that Barnett and Johnson had made secret deals to admit Meredith, while promising publicly never to surrender. The people of Mississippi believed Paul Johnson had remained faithful to "our way of life" and elected him to the state's highest office.[1]

Like a terrible swift sword, change came to Mississippi in the early 1960s and Governor Johnson wisely and courageously counseled Mississippians to accept that change. In his inaugural address on January 21, 1964, he said, "Hate or prejudice or ignorance will not lead Mississippi while I sit in the governor's chair...if I must fight, it will not be a rear-guard defense of yesterday...it will be an all out assault for our share of tomorrow." He concluded that remarkable address with an impromptu, "God bless everyone of you, all Mississippians, black and white, here and away from home."[2]

Governor Johnson's inaugural received high praise, but his powers of expression were greater than his powers of persuasion, and many Mississippians would not give up their defense of yesterday. That was especially true of some members on the College Board, which played a major role in shaping Mississippi's response to change in the 1960s. That Mississippi would bleed in the wake of the terrible swift sword was inevitable, but perhaps it bled more than it had to, in part because of the policies and procedures of the Board of Trustees of Mississippi Institutions of Higher Learning. There was an indication that the College Board would fight a rear guard defense of yesterday even before the governor had formed the phrase.[3]

Mississippi State University won the Southeastern Conference basketball championship in February 1963 and a berth in the NCAA tournament. In the early pairings, State was scheduled to play Loyola University of Chicago, a team with several black players. If Mississippi State played Loyola, the "unwritten law" would be broken. The unwritten law prohibited Mississippi's white institutions from playing integrated teams and was formulated after Jones County Junior College played an integrated football team in the Little Rose Bowl of 1955. It was first invoked in 1959 to prevent the Ole Miss baseball team from advancing to the NCAA tournament after it had won the SEC title. A board member declared that athletic competition with integrated teams was the "greatest threat" to Mississippi's way of life since Reconstruction.[4]

Mississippi State had won the SEC basketball championship in 1962, but because of the unwritten law did not advance to the NCAA tournament. When Mississippi State again won the championship in 1963, President Dean W. Colvard and Coach James "Babe" McCarthy announced that State would play in the NCAA tournament. Following President Colvard's announcement, the Board of Trustees held a called meeting on Saturday March 9, 1963. At that meeting, M. M. Roberts offered a resolution forbidding State to play in the tournament. After his motion failed, Roberts introduced a motion to dismiss President Colvard. Following a brief but bitter exchange between Roberts and Verner Holmes, the board gave President Colvard a vote of confidence, which in effect repealed the "unwritten law."[5]

After the meeting, a disconsolate Roberts told the press, "It looks like we are about to lose our Southern way of life" and confessed that he had prayed for State to lose its last two games "because I knew we would be faced with this problem." In a last desperate effort to save "our way of life," a judge in Jones County issued an injunction prohibiting the Mississippi State basketball team from leaving the state. As soon as President Colvard was advised of the court's action, he and Coach McCarthy left the state to prevent the injunction from being served. With President Colvard in Alabama, and "Babe" McCarthy in Tennessee, both safely beyond the reach of the injunction, the team left Starkville on schedule without incident.[6]

Some board members were emotionally unable to accept the changes that were taking place all around them. At the beginning of the "long, hot summer" of 1964, when college students from across America came to Mississippi to conduct freedom schools and registration drives, the board directed college presidents to report any suspicious looking characters on their campuses to the governor's office. The "exploding tension" of that summer also prompted the board to adopt new rules restricting the use of college facilities by the general public. Under the new regulations that were invoked for the first time at the Ole Miss-Memphis State football game at Oxford on September 19, 1964, the parents of black football players from Memphis State were not allowed to eat in the Ole Miss commons and white cafeteria workers, who had been deputized, were directed to arrest any blacks if they attempted to use the dining facilities on game day.[7]

Two days before the game, a board member introduced two resolutions to deal with that "serious situation." In his first resolution, he recommended that no new contracts be made with integrated teams unless they agreed to leave all black players, students, employees, and faculty members at home when the games were played in Mississippi. His second resolution directed Chancellor Williams not to admit any "agitators" to the Memphis State game and further directed him to tell the president of Memphis State to exclude "agitators and troublemakers" from their section of the stadium. After both resolutions were tabled, a board member who voted against tabling the motions, then suggested that black Memphis State fans could be stopped by the Highway Patrol at the city limits and not allowed to enter Oxford to attend the game. No action was taken on that proposal and the game was played on schedule without incident. The parents of the black players who were turned away from the cafeteria also left without incident.[8]

The board's resistance to change and its defense of yesterday inevitably entangled it in personnel matters. The doctrinaire members of the board were determined to prevent the appointment of professors they believed to be a threat to Mississippi's way of life. The board's antipathy for subversive professors was heightened in the fall of 1963 when James W. Silver of Ole Miss delivered his presidential address to the Southern Historical Association. Professor Silver's address, titled "Mississippi: The Closed Society," angered several members of the board, especially M. M. Roberts, and many other state officials. Mississippi's power structure was in near unanimous agreement that Silver was a threat and should be dismissed from the Ole Miss faculty. Following his speech, the board appointed a committee, chaired by M. M. Roberts to gather evidence that could be used to dismiss Silver from his tenured position as professor of history, a position he had held since 1936.[9]

As the Board of Trustees was conducting its investigation of Professor Silver, which included private detectives who followed him to speaking engagements, the Mississippi legislature also took up the Silver issue. A state representative introduced a resolution demanding Silver's dismissal and pledged himself to any course of action short of violence to oust the professor. Another legislator who conceded that Silver's dismissal would enhance his reputation in the North said that should no longer be a consideration: "It is better that he get national fame than for us to receive social death." The senator added if the University would not fire Silver, the legislature should.[10]

While the legislature was fulminating, the Board of Trustees filed a set of charges against Professor Silver on April 27, 1964. Silver informed executive Secretary Jobe that his counsel would respond to the charges. Before any final resolution was made of the charges against him, Professor Silver asked for and received a leave of absence to accept a visiting professorship at Notre Dame University. Following that year at Notre Dame, Professor Silver did not return to the University, although he wanted to. University officials indicated to Professor Silver that it would be best if he did not come back to Oxford. Silver remained at Notre Dame for another year and then moved to the University of South Florida, where he retired in 1978. Years later, Professor Silver recalled those troubled times and said, "I don't blame Roberts or the Board. They thought they were defending their heritage, and hell, they were." When asked how he would like to be remembered, Silver said, "I just want to be remembered as someone who helped change Mississippi."[11]

Although Professor Silver's case is the most celebrated, it is only one of many similar cases involving academic freedom at Mississippi's institutions of higher learning in the 1960s and 1970s. The list is lengthy and includes Corrine T. Carpenter of Alcorn College, Kenneth Rainey of Jackson State, Michael Trister, George Strickler, and Russell Barrett of the University of Mississippi, and W. D. Norwood, Monte Piliawsky, and Sanford Wood of the University of Southern Mississippi.[12]

The underlying cause of the difficulty between the College Board and liberal college professors was that the board was dominated by two or three men of extremely conservative ideology in the 1960s. Those board members did not just resist change, they manipulated board policy to promote their own ideology. In 1951, the board adopted a policy that required faculty members to resign if they ran for public office. The board reaffirmed that policy on August 19, 1971. However, on April 20, 1972, the board exempted Carl Butler from that policy and allowed him to complete the spring semester while a candidate for congress. Professor Butler was a political science professor at Mississippi State University who ran as a Republican against Democratic incumbent, David Bowen, who defeated Butler by a vote of nearly two to one.[13]

Perhaps an even more significant example of the manipulation of board policy in defense of yesterday was the board's infamous speaker ban. When the board was informed that Robert Kennedy had been invited to speak at Ole Miss on March 20, 1966, M. M. Roberts introduced a resolution declaring his appearance "an affront" to the Board of Trustees and demanded that the invitation be withdrawn. Although the board did not rescind Kennedy's invitation, it did adopt a more restrictive speaker policy in November 1966 that required college presidents to personally approve off campus speakers.

The new speaker policy was first invoked at Ole Miss in May 1967 when Chancellor Williams announced that Aaron Henry would not be allowed to speak on campus. Following Chancellor Williams' ruling, the Ole Miss chapter of the American Association of University Professors filed a federal suit asking that the speaker ban be set aside as a violation of first amendment rights. The federal district court ruled that the existing policy was unconstitutional and ordered the Board of Trustees to draft a new speaker policy. Nine months later, a three judge panel rejected the board's new speaker policy, which was actually more restrictive than the policy it superseded. In its ruling, the court gave the board the option of either accepting the court's regulations or having no regulations at all. The board accepted the court's regulations, which gave college presidents, with the advice and consent of a campus review committee, the final authority to approve or disapprove outside speakers. Perhaps in any other state, the court's final decree would have ended the controversy over the speaker ban. That was not the case in Mississippi.

On February 7, 1970, the Mississippi State University Young Democrats invited Mayor Charles Evers of Fayette to speak on the campus later in the spring. President William Giles approved the request. On March 4, Executive Secretary E. E. Thrash wrote President Giles informing him that the board, by a vote of 12 to 1, had directed him to withdraw the invitation to Charles Evers. Verner Holmes cast the lone vote against overruling President Giles. The board cited Evers' involvement in a student demonstration at Alcorn in 1966 as the reason for its disapproval. President Giles, with the approval of the Mississippi State Speakers Review Committee, disregarded the board's directive and approved the request to bring Evers to the campus. Two days later, the Board of Trustees, acting on the insistence of M. M. Roberts, invoked its power as the governing authority of Mississippi State University and ordered President Giles to disallow Mayor Evers from speaking on the Mississippi State campus. President Giles obeyed the order and withdrew his approval of Evers' speech. The next day, claiming that Roberts and the Board of Trustees had acted "in open and complete contempt of the dignity and authority" of the federal district court, the Young Democrats filed a motion asking for injunctive relief and a contempt citation against the Board of Trustees. On March 9, Federal District Judge William Keady granted a restraining order permitting Evers to speak, but declined to issue contempt citations against Roberts or the Board of Trustees.

During the heated controversy over Evers' appearance at Mississippi State University, President Giles received a telephone call from M. M. Roberts, who was extremely angry at President Giles and distraught over the prospect that Charles Evers was going to speak at Mississippi State. Roberts became increasingly upset as the conversation proceeded and eventually lost his composure and cursed the president and swore that he would see that he was fired. On the day after Mayor Evers' speech, Roberts wrote a now famous letter to the members of the Board of Trustees. After making some very disparaging remarks about the administration at Mississippi State, Roberts added a handwritten postscript: "The letter was written after some thought and registers my sincere views. We are in troubled times."

About ten days after this letter was written, the board met for its regular monthly meeting and Roberts attempted to carry out his threat against President Giles. He repeated some of the statements he had made in the letter and asked the board to dismiss President Giles. In a bitter rebuttal, Verner Holmes defended Giles and reminded board members that Giles was under court order and he had no alternative but to obey the law. Holmes' reasoned and impassioned assessment convinced the board that any further intercession was unwise and the board then distanced itself from the speaker ban controversy, and took no action on Roberts' proposal to dismiss President Giles.[14]

Long after the speaker ban controversy had subsided, President Giles remembered the students who had sued him and the board: "I had a lot fonder feeling for those young people who sued me than they ever guessed I did. [I] would have been part of a conspiracy had I called them in and said, Look, fellows, you can go to court and do this and that. But you could stand by and approve of what they were doing silently. But you see, they never could know this." They do now, if they have read this far.[15]

The speaker ban and many of the board's other policies during the 1960s and 1970s were shaped by its obsessive fear of campus violence and the presumption that integration would lead to chaos and disorder. The kind of campus violence the board had most feared occurred in May 1970 at Jackson State College. The violence at Jackson State was different from the unrest at Alcorn and Mississippi Valley and did not stem from discontent with academic policies or dissatisfaction with Jackson State President John Peoples. The roots of that riot ran much deeper. A member of the President's Commission on Campus Unrest cited the "historic pattern of racism" as the fundamental cause of the Jackson State riot.[16]

Jackson State is located on Lynch Street, which was then a major thoroughfare through the campus connecting a white residential section in west Jackson to the downtown business district. Sometimes in the spring, Jackson State students would gather along Lynch Street and taunt whites as they drove through the campus. In 1965 and 1966, there were minor incidents of rock-throwing, and in the spring of 1968, Martin Luther King's assassination provoked a more serious demonstration. Jackson police were ordered to the campus and used tear gas to restore order. Fifteen people were arrested. There was also a minor demonstration in 1969.[17]

On May 13, 1970, a small group of Jackson State students began pelting passing cars with rocks in the late afternoon and early evening. As the crowd grew, the Jackson police department established a road block on Lynch Street and Jackson Mayor Russell Davis requested Governor John Bell Williams to mobilize a local National Guard unit and place the Mississippi highway patrol on standby in case they were needed.

The next night, a larger and more restive group of students congregated along Lynch Street and Jackson police sealed off the street. While the students were milling about, a rumor began to spread among the growing crowd that Charles Evers and his wife had been killed. That rumor excited the restless students and a truck was set afire. Students began hurling rocks and bricks at white policemen and highway patrolmen who were stationed along Lynch Street. Shortly after midnight, the crashing sound of breaking glass, which coincided with the arrival of an armored riot-control vehicle, provoked a 28 second fusillade toward Alexander Hall, a woman's dormitory. Two students were killed and twelve others were wounded. The deaths of James Earl Green and Phillip L. Gibbs prompted shock and anger in the black community of Jackson and throughout Mississippi. President John Peoples said the students were slain "wantonly and determinedly." The *Blue and White Flash*, the Jackson State student newspaper, called the shooting "pure slaughter."

The Board of Trustees deplored the death of the two students and closed Jackson State for the rest of the spring semester. Mayor Davis, in an unprecedented move, appointed a biracial committee to investigate the incident. Governor Williams, although he issued a formal statement deploring the tragic deaths, refused to cooperate with Mayor Davis' investigation. Jackson policemen and the city's newspapers claimed that snipers had provoked the burst of gunfire and blamed the deaths of the two students on the "toll of [student] misconduct." Student representatives from several Mississippi colleges and universities issued statements criticizing local public officials and especially the Jackson press for justifying the shooting of college students.[18]

Following the riots at Kent State in Ohio and Jackson State, President Richard Nixon appointed a presidential commission to study campus unrest that had occurred on college campuses throughout the country. The President's Commission on Campus Unrest visited Jackson State and conducted a thorough investigation. The Commission concluded that "the stark fact underlying all other causes of student unrest [at Jackson State College] is the historic pattern of racism that substantially affects daily life in Mississippi."

According to Steven Lesher, a member of the President's Commission, the academic deficiencies of Mississippi's black colleges had a devastating effect on blacks in Mississippi. He said "a recycling of unsophisticated rural blacks through under-financed colleges where they are taught, by people from similar circumstances, to teach yet another generation of the disadvantaged is like the hamster on an exercise wheel who races to escape but gets nowhere." Lesher found that black college presidents were intimidated by the white power structure who viewed their efforts to upgrade black schools with suspicion if not hostility. Black college presidents were thus forced to serve two masters, their black constituency, which would no longer accept things as they were, and the white power structure that governed their institutions and would not allow them or their colleges to become engines of change.

When the President's Commission published its findings, Governor Williams and Attorney General A. F. Summer dismissed the report as the work of a "kangaroo court." Echoing their sentiment was Congressman G. V. Montgomery who also claimed that the report was prejudiced against Mississippi. Few white Mississippians, especially members of the Board of Trustees of Institutions of Higher Learning, were willing to accept any responsibility or blame for the deaths that occurred at Jackson State College.[19]

One white Mississippian, Oliver Emmerich, stood almost alone in his assessment of the causes of the Jackson State riot. The former member of the Board of Trustees, and editor of the *McComb Enterprise*, identified a complex set of circumstances that he said, in culmination, triggered the violence at Jackson State. Emmerich cited the board's long standing policy of banning speakers from Mississippi's institutions of higher learning; the racial dimension of almost every official public policy; the continued refusal of the state's political leadership to appoint blacks to the public agencies that affect their daily lives; and the fact that white policemen fear no recrimination for killing blacks. Emmerich also reported that Governor Williams and Mayor Davis were at loggerheads over what had happened at Jackson State, and who had been responsible for firing the shots that killed the two students, a question that remains unanswered.[20]

It is historically significant that while there were serious racial disturbances on college campuses in the spring of 1970, Mississippi's public school system was implementing the most sweeping racial integration in the state's educational history. During the spring semester of 1970, Mississippi's dual, segregated school system was superseded by a unified, integrated system and black and white children went to school together with unexpected success. The integration of the public school system was achieved more peacefully than almost anyone believed possible. Unlike the Board of Trustees of Institutions of Higher Learning, Mississippi's classroom teachers and school officials focused their energy on acceptance of change rather than resistance to change. They too, according to historian Jack Bass, were "unlikely heroes."

At no other time in its troubled history has higher education been more directly influenced by an individual board member than it was in the 1960s and 1970s. The most doctrinaire member of the Board of Trustees, and in some ways its most influential member, was M. M. Roberts of Hattiesburg. As the acknowledged "Mississippi Southern board member," Roberts was the driving force behind the realignment of the traditional pecking order among the state institutions of higher learning. Two years after he joined the Board of Trustees, Mississippi Southern College was elevated to university status in 1962, and under his influence a new funding formula was adopted in 1964. The new formula was numerically driven and almost immediately elevated the University of Southern Mississippi to a funding level equal to Mississippi State and Ole Miss, and paved the way for USM's designation as a comprehensive university and its authorization to grant doctoral degrees.[21]

M. M. Roberts exercised his enormous influence on board policy through a strategy that he devised soon after becoming a member of the board:
Let me tell you, I always tied in with either State or Ole Miss, because with [one of] them, and what votes I could get outside of it, I could do something...if I made up my mind what I wanted to do. I had to get that crowd, I'm telling you about the manipulations...and that's the reason you have so many 7-6 votes.[22]

Like some other board members over the years, M. M. Roberts did not have a sense of humor, or a sense of history, and it was difficult for him to keep things in perspective. In the springtime hijinx of college students, Roberts saw a dark conspiracy, and in the naive idealism of youth, he saw a creeping socialism. He did not understand that those college kids who came to Mississippi in the summer of 1964 brought with them a belief in the freedom of the human spirit that is this nation's surest safeguard against communism, fascism, or atheism. He failed to realize that those young people were not unlike the young men and women of Mississippi, except that their social consciousness had been awakened to injustice and racial discrimination.

The 1960s was a time of confrontation and change, and one of the most interesting confrontations in Mississippi during those years occurred in the closed meetings of the College Board, between Verner Smith Holmes and M. M. Roberts. Holmes was physician who served on the College Board for twenty-four years from 1956 to1980. He had a great sense of humor, an innate sense of fairness, and a profound sense of history. His sense of history gave him a perspective that few other board members had, and enabled him to say: "I look back now, and I am ashamed of the way I voted sometimes, you know you make so many mistakes. I think back in those days we all, in our hearts, were a little racist."[23]

In those troubled times, Holmes was not a liberal but a realist who recognized that Mississippi and the College Board and the institutions it governed could not escape the changes taking place everywhere else in America. He was also a pragmatist and preferred the most direct and the least painful route to change. When the federal court ordered the desegregation of the university hospital, Holmes and Dean Robert Marston of the medical center were discussing the removal of the WHITE and COLORED signs from the hospital's entrances. Dean Marston asked Holmes, "Should I bring it to the Board?" Holmes replied, "My God, no!" Holmes and Martston took the signs down at midnight on the day before the court order was to go into effect. Holmes remembered, "We were kind of disappointed that nobody even noticed it. You know," he reflected, "a lot of times if you just do things, people would accept them and not create a great controversy over them."[24]

People may not have noticed that those signs were gone, but there were two changes during the 1960s and early 1970s that could not go unnoticed. One of those changes was the fact that the students and the faculties of Mississippi's state institutions of higher learning were integrated.

As significant as those changes were, there was an even more dramatic changing of the guard on the Board of Trustees. In 1972, Ross Barnett's appointees, including M. M. Roberts, rotated off the board and for the first time ever, an African American was appointed to the College Board, and for the first time in many years a woman would serve on the Board of Trustees of State Institutions of Higher Learning.

The election of Governor Bill Waller in 1971 and his appointments to the College Board were an announcement that Mississippi's Closed Society was opening up.

Chapter 9 — Higher Educatiion in Troubled Times, 1963-1972

Footnotes Chapter 9

1 For an account of this period, see McLemore [ed.], *History of Mississippi*, II, Neil McMillan, Chapter 28, "Development of Civil Rights, 1956-1970," 154-176; see also John Ditmar, *Local People, The Struggle for Civil Rights in Mississippi*, (1994) and Erle Johnston, *Mississippi's Defiant Years, 1953-1973* (1990).

2 McArthur, *Inaugural Addresses 1890-1980*, 327-333; see also Claude Sitton, *New York Times*, January 22, 1964.

3 For a general study of this period, see Neil McMillen, *The Citizens' Council, Organized Resistance to the Second Reconstruction, 1954-1964* (Urbana, 1971).

4 *Clarion-Ledger*, March 10, 1963; *Minutes*, April 18, 1963; interview with M. M. Roberts on September 23, 1978 at Hattiesburg, Mississippi.

5 *Daily Mississippian*, February 21, 1963, March 6, 1963, March 7, 1963; *Minutes*, February 21, 1963; for a discussion of this episode, see Dean Wallace Colvard, *Mixed Emotions* (1985), 41-95, 156; the minutes of the March 9 board meeting were not included in the published minutes of the board; see *Jackson Daily News-The Clarion-Ledger*, March 10, 1963; Roberts Interview; Holmes and Jobe Interviews; *Commercial Appeal*, March 10, 1963; see also *Clarion-Ledger*, March 15, 1983, for a twenty year retrospective article on this event.

6 Colvard, *Mixed Emotions*, 41-95; *Clarion-Ledger*, March 15, 1983.

7 AAUP *Bulletin*, Autumn, 1965, 347; Silver, *The Closed Society*, 319-320; for accounts of that summer, see Leon Holt, *The Summer That Didn't End* (1965), Tracy Sugarman, *Stranger at the Gates, A Summer in Mississippi* (1966), and Sally Belfrage, *Freedom Summer* (1966).

8 AAUP *Bulletin*; *Minutes*, September 17, 1964.

9 *Minutes*, November 21, 1963; interview with Professor James W. Silver on March 16-17, 1982 at Dunedin, Florida; a transcript of this interview is in the Holmes Collection.

10 *Clarion-Ledger*, April 1, 1964, *Commercial Appeal*, March 28, 1964.

11 For Professor Silver's perspective on these issues, see James W. Silver, *Running Scared, Silver in Mississippi* (1984), Chapters 4, 5, 6, and Appendix F; for an assessment of the Silver Case, see AAUP *Bulletin*, Autumn 1965, 351-355.

12 AAUP *Bulletin*, Autumn 1962, 248-252, *Times Picayune*, October 10, 1962; *Jackson Daily News*, September 7, 1970; *Minutes*, January 18, 1972; *Daily Mississippian*, January 9, February 11, 12, 1970; AAUP *Bulletin*, Spring 1970, 76-80; see also Ken Vinson, "Mississippi: Signs of Life, The Lawyers of Ole Miss," *The Nation* (June 23, 1969), 791-793; *Minutes*, January 15, 1970; *Clarion-Ledger*, December 29, 1970; see also Monte Piliawsky, *Exit 13, Oppression and Racism in Academia* (1982), Chapter 8, "Faculty Firings: The Permanent Purge," 76-92.

13 *Minutes*, March 21, 1957, August 19, 1971, and April 20, 1972.

14 For a study of the speaker ban controversy, see Lucie Robertson Bridgforth, "'Bomb the Ban,'A Study of the Legal Controversy Surrounding Off-Campus Speakers at Mississippi Institutions of Higher Learning," (M.A. thesis, University of Mississippi, 1979); a transcript of an interview with President William Giles at Starkville, Mississippi, on May 30, 1979 is in the Holmes Collection; see also John Carter, "A Boll Weevil Six Feet Long," *Library Journal* (October 15, 1969), 3615-3619; a copy of Roberts' Letter to All Members of the Board, March 10, 1970, is in the Holmes Collection; for President Giles' expression of his appreciation to Verner Holmes for his support, see Giles to Holmes, March 20, 1970, in Holmes Collection; see also William C. Keady, *All Rise, Memoirs of a Mississippi Federal Judge* (1988).

15 See transcripts of Giles Interview in the Homes Collection.

16 For an analysis of the Jackson State riot, see William W. Scranton, Chairman, The President's Commission on Campus Unrest, *The Report of the President's Commission on Campus Unrest, Including Special Reports: The Killings at Jackson State, The Kent State Tragedy* (1970), 411-465; for a brief account of the riot, see Rhodes, *Jackson State,* 176-180.

17 Ibid.

18 *New York Times*, May 16, 23, 1970; *Jackson Daily News*, May 15, 19, 1970; *Minutes*, May 21, June 18, 1970; see also John R. Salter, *Jackson, Mississippi: An American Chronicle of Struggle and Schism* (1979).

19 Scranton, *President's Commission on Campus Violence,* 444; Stephen Lesher, "Jackson State a Year After," *New York Times Magazine* (March 21, 1971), 56; on the increasing militancy among Mississippi black college students, see Anne Moody, *Coming of Age in Mississippi* (1968); *Clarion-Ledger*, October 20, 1970, August 27, 1970.

20 *McComb Enterprise Journal,* October 7, 1970.

21 Roberts Interview.

22 Ibid.

23 Holmes Interview.

24 Ibid; interview with President Robert Marston, University of Florida, Gainesville, Florida on March 18, 1982.

Chapter 10
Governing a System of Universities, 1972-2000

The early period of the twenty-first century is likely to be one of the most troubling in the history of the nation's higher education.

Aims C. McGuinness

After Mississippi emerged from the crisis of integration and the days of dissent, its institutions of higher learning continued to be the focus of controversy. The primary issue was the duplication of courses and degree programs in Mississippi's eight public universities. Legislative critics and public officials claimed that Mississippi's institutions of higher learning were trying to do too much with too little, with the unintended consequence that its colleges and universities were mediocre if not marginal. Support for coordination of degree programs, which had gone unheeded for three decades, eventually gave way to a demand for the consolidation or closure of some of Mississippi's state institutions of higher learning.

Increasing support for a coordinated state system of universities in Mississippi was consistent with an increasing national awareness that the proliferation of colleges and universities since World War II had created a "basic and inescapable need" for some kind of coordination of American higher education. In 1971, Robert Berdahl, author of *Statewide Coordination of Higher Education*, argued that academic freedom did not depend necessarily on institutional autonomy and "that the state's funding and interest in higher education legitimately permitted it some substantial voice in such major decisions as approving new campuses and new degree programs." Berdahl considered coordination inevitable, and the only question was how and by what agencies would coordination be implemented. He preferred that it be done by a state governing board, otherwise "it would occur by default at the less educationally informed and more politicized level of the governor's office or legislative staff."[1]

That issue was joined in Mississippi when Governor William Waller, who was inaugurated in 1972, appointed a blue ribbon committee to study higher education, specifically the need to coordinate degree programs and the feasibility of consolidating or closing some of the state's institutions of higher learning. When the committee published its report, which was critical of higher education, the president of the Board of Trustees, Thomas Turner, disavowed the report:"This is the governor's report." The committee criticized the state's public universities because they did not train their graduates for jobs that were available in Mississippi. President Turner discounted that claim altogether. "I think it's the state of Mississippi's obligation," he said, "to put jobs here for the people we turn out."[2]

Some members of the Board of Trustees were offended by the criticism of Governor Waller's committee, but rather than acknowledging the need to reevaluate its policies and priorities during a period of retrenchment, the board "circled the wagons" and refused to cooperate with Governor Waller and his committee on higher education. Because of that intransigence the Board of Trustees and its staff, according to Eugene Hickok, "became more vulnerable to institutional, governmental, and public criticism."[3]

The first indication that the College Board would be forced to reorder its priorities came in February 1974 when Governor Waller vetoed a special catch-up appropriation for university libraries. Governor Waller explained that he vetoed the library bill to force the Board of Trustees to divert money from capital outlays to operational expenses. Because college enrollment had leveled off, Governor Waller argued, huge expenditures for capital construction were not a judicious use of the state's financial resources. He insisted that his veto would not damage higher education because the $65.1 million regular appropriation was sufficient to meet the actual needs of higher education. In his veto message, Governor Waller also criticized the College Board's allocation formula. He said that the enrollment driven formula had encouraged the smaller colleges to duplicate popular programs to attract students.[4]

Eight months after Governor Waller's veto of the library bill, additional evidence indicated that the growth cycle had peaked. In October 1974, the state Building Commission imposed a moratorium, on construction preplanning at the state's institutions of higher learning. During the moratorium the Building Commission staff would review the construction priorities as established by higher education officials. The Board of Trustees reacted angrily to that mandate, claiming it was an infringement upon its constitutional authority. During the next several months, relations between the board and the commission deteriorated. But even the College Board, despite its reaction to the commission's moratorium, had become convinced that capital construction must be curtailed and instructed the board staff to study carefully the requests for new buildings to determine if the requests were justified. That directive was a prelude to retrenchment, and it was the first indication that the board realized that the postwar college boom had run its course.[5]

Boards of Trustees of Institutions of Higher Learning had been a part of Mississippi's power elite since the end of Reconstruction and had traditionally conducted the affairs of higher education in secret, closed door sessions far removed from the glare and stare of public opinion. Aided by the secrecy that cloaked its actions, and abetted by its constitutional independence, the Board of Trustees, as Governor Waller claimed, had for many years exercised its authority with arrogance. Having come of age in the Closed Society, most board members who served during the 1970s were uncomfortable with the direction the open society was taking.

When the Mississippi State University student newspaper asked board president Boswell Stevens if he would support inter-dormitory visitation, Stevens responded with an arrogance that must have amused more than it offended: "I think all of them [boys and girls] should just live together." Stevens then exclaimed that he was against dormitory visitation and he would never vote for it as long as he was on the board, and criticized the *Reflector* for using a university telephone to conduct such a frivolous interview. He finally said he was "tired of all this bullshit" and hung up the telephone.[6]

President of the powerful Mississippi Farm Bureau Federation, Boswell Stevens was one of three presidents of the College Board during the 1970s that did not have a college degree. The other two were Tommy Turner and Milton Brister. Stevens' disdain for student opinion and his obstinacy in the face of a changing society was more or less shared by most other trustees and generated cynicism among Mississippi's student constituency. An amusing expression of that cynicism was a cartoon in the University of Southern Mississippi's *Student Printz* showing two board members playing high stakes poker. One said to the other: "I see your vet school...and raise you a sci tech building."[7]

The Board of Trustees also had an unflattering record during the 1970s of partiality toward certain institutions. The most striking example is Jackson State University's request to build a $100,000 memorial garden to its past presidents. That request, made on May 18, 1978, provoked an acrimonious and protracted debate. Even though the legislature had already appropriated the funds for the garden, and the state building commission had already authorized the expenditure, and even after President John Peoples had announced that construction on the project would soon begin, several board members insisted on cancelling or at least scaling back the project. They claimed that such a large expenditure was not a justifiable use of Mississippi's educational resources during a period of retrenchment. As the debate intensified board member Verner Holmes questioned a colleague, "Don't you know that if the president of the University of Mississippi or Mississippi State was asking for something, we wouldn't do this to them?" The colleague responded, "Well, maybe not." The board members opposing the memorial garden, according to Holmes, "were hell bent" against it, but finally relented and allowed its construction.

Verner Holmes' claim that similar requests from Ole Miss or Mississippi State would not trigger such rigid scrutiny was documented on January 17, 1980, when the board authorized the renovation of a dean's office at the University of Mississippi. The request to renovate that one office at a cost of $26,000, more than one-fourth of the total Jackson State expenditure, did not elicit even a passing comment when the board unanimously approved it.[8]

The College Board's preferences and predilections often produced headlines and the Mississippi media accused the board of being utterly indifferent to public opinion. For years the press had assailed the board for conducting public business behind closed doors, and in the 1970s the media stepped up its campaign to gain admission to board meetings. The board held steadfast, however, and kept its meetings closed but in doing so it undermined its credibility. Eventually, the legislature passed an open meetings law and the Board of Trustees, and all other state agencies, were required to conduct their business in public sessions. The College Board fought the issue all the way to the State Supreme Court.

By the end of the 1970s the business of higher education in Mississippi was not only being conducted in meetings open to the public, but higher education itself had become a vast and complex public enterprise. The modern twentieth century institutions of higher learning bore little resemblance to the Old Time Colleges, or their post-Civil War predecessors. The new universities were local industries with huge payrolls. University presidents functioned as CEOs. Deans and department heads were mid-level management. The newest and best equipment first found its way to the business office and the physical plant, and then to the laboratory and classroom. The hub of the campus shifted subtly from the library to the admissions office. College officials began playing the numbers game. The public at large and the legislature in particular had come to expect the new CEOs of higher education to make decisions on the basis of economics, as well as academics. And the legislature was more determined than ever to hold Mississippi's governing board accountable for those decisions.

The relationship between the Board of Trustees and the legislature had rarely ever been harmonious, even during the decades of growth and expansion. But during the period of retrenchment in the late twentieth century, that relationship soured and the legislature became increasingly critical of what it considered to be wasteful duplication. However, while the legislature was mandating the elimination of unnecessary duplication, the lawmakers themselves yielded to local interests, and in 1974, the Mississippi legislature elevated the five state colleges to university status and ignored its own mandate against proliferation by establishing a Dental School at the University of Mississippi Medical Center, and a School of Architecture and a School of Veterinary Medicine at Mississippi State.

Nevertheless, the Board of Trustees was forced to respond to the mounting criticism that academic entrepreneurs were squandering Mississippi's educational resources, and in an effort to curtail the proliferation and duplication of new degree programs, the board directed the eight institutions to conduct an academic inventory and identify all degree programs that were not accredited. The board also directed university officials to initiate long-range planning studies that would assess the future needs and goals of Mississippi's institutions of higher learning. The board required each institution to file its intent to establish a new program ninety days before it was to start and to explain how the program was related to the "stated purposes" of that institution.[9]

But as Joseph Gibson so aptly said in 1945, "eternal vigilance" is the price the board must pay to restrict the proliferation of new programs. Board members met only once every thirty days, but academicians could meet thirty times every day if necessary to plan and plot a strategy to justify new programs.

After the academic inventories had been completed and the long range studies had been made, the Board of Trustees began consolidating and eliminating marginal programs. On February 20, 1975, the board reported to the legislature that the universities were having "surprising success in reducing duplication," and that one hundred unaccredited or unproductive programs had been discontinued. Some legislators, however, saw the board's "surprising success" as too little and too late. Senator Theodore Smith of Corinth called for more paring of degree programs, noting that the University of Mississippi offered more graduate programs than Harvard University.[10]

Six months after submitting its report to the legislature, the Board of Trustees denied a request by Jackson State to begin a doctoral program in education. The board's action brought a sharp and surprising response. The *Clarion-Ledger* reported that the board denied the request because there were already similar programs at State, Southern, and Ole Miss and quoted the deans at those institutions as saying that all three of the existing programs were necessary, but that one more program was not necessary. The Executive Secretary of the Board of Trustees explained that new degree programs were approved only after the board staff had thoroughly studied the request and had determined that the new program was not an "unnecessary duplication" of an existing program. But the *Clarion-Ledger* was not impressed with that explanation and accused certain board members of serving as "cheerleaders" for their favored institutions. Senator Jim Noblin of Jackson accused the board of denying Jackson State's request because its program would draw students from the other three institutions. He also took note that the deans of the schools where the doctoral programs already existed had said that three were not too many, but that four was one too many.[11]

The controversy over Jackson State's doctoral program was only a skirmish in the impending battle over doctoral consolidation. The larger question of doctoral programs and doctoral consolidation was brought before the board in January 1976 when the board staff proposed a consolidation plan that assigned doctoral programs exclusively to Mississippi State, Southern Mississippi, and Ole Miss. Primarily the work of the board staff, the plan came as a complete surprise to university presidents, and even to some board members. In presenting the proposal to the board, Executive Secretary E. E. Thrash reported that there were nineteen doctoral programs that had only one student currently enrolled, fourteen had only two students, and ten had only three students. Under the original plan, the number of doctorates would be reduced from 103 to 77. After a lengthy discussion, the board postponed any action for thirty days to allow the university presidents to study the effect of doctoral consolidation and report their findings and recommendations to the board. Dr. Robert Harrison, the only African American on the board, voted in favor of postponement because he and several other board members had not been told about the consolidation plan until it was brought to the board for a vote. Dr. Harrison insisted that "any proposal this serious should be given to the Board in writing seven days prior to the meeting at which it is formally presented." Thus, the first of a series of delays occurred, and over the next several months, the doctoral consolidation program was drastically modified.[12]

The board's effort to consolidate existing doctoral programs and correlate new programs to the "stated purposes" of each institution presupposed a clear statement of the role and scope of Mississippi's eight institutions of higher learning. But there was no such instrument and on July 15, 1976, the Board of Trustees began formulating a comprehensive, long range role and scope plan for each of the eight universities under its governance. Those role and scope statements were nearly five years in the making.[13]

On March 15, 1979, the president of the Board of Trustees reviewed a proposed draft of the statement, but informed the board that it would undergo further revision before it was presented for a final vote.[14]

A week after the board made the proposed role and scope statement public, the Academy for Educational Development, a Washington consulting firm that had been retained by the legislature to study higher education in Mississippi, published a report highly critical of program duplication at Mississippi's eight institutions. Based on its assessment of an impending enrollment decline and budget constraints, the Academy issued a stern warning to the Board of Trustees:

> To date, the philosophy of the Board of Trustees has been to delegate almost all planning and management responsibilities to the institutions…The Board must exert a will to lead…and define the mission of each institution.[15]

Armed with the findings of the Academy Study, the legislature prodded the board to reduce unnecessary duplication and mandated role and scope assignments to the eight universities. The board was already moving in that direction and during the next few months, the term "role and scope" gave way to a more euphemistic term, "mission statement." The mission statements for each institution were finally completed and adopted by the board on November 18, 1981. The statements were drafted by a special board committee and published in the spring of 1982, with an accompanying document titled "Official Explanation."[16]

At the time the mission statements were announced, the board also mandated a review of all degree programs and indicated that the role and scope assignments might be modified after those reviews had been completed. This new round of program reviews was a continuation of an earlier policy and eventually resulted in the deletion or suspension of a large number of degree programs and a significant reduction of doctoral programs.

The mission statements divided the eight universities into three categories. The University of Mississippi, Mississippi State University, and the University of Southern Mississippi were designated as comprehensive universities. All three universities would continue to offer doctoral programs, but each institution was assigned leadership roles in specific disciplines.

Jackson State was classified as an urban university. Its primary mission was "to engage in more organized research that is directly related to the urban area of Jackson."

The other four institutions, Alcorn, Delta State, Mississippi Valley, and Mississippi University for Women, were classified as regional universities. Those institutions would continue to offer their existing baccalaureate programs and some graduate programs.[17]

In 1983, the Board of Trustees adopted a plan to promote "excellence" in a number of carefully selected and limited academic disciplines at the three comprehensive universities. The "Centers of Academic Excellence" were correlated to the leadership roles assigned to each university and were established as follows:[18]

Mississippi State University
    Biological Sciences, Engineering, Food Science, Technology

University of Mississippi
   Chemistry, History, Physics, English

University of Southern Mississippi
   Communications (Journalism), Computer Science, Marine Science

A year later, the Board of Trustees reassigned the leadership role in journalism from the University of Southern Mississippi to the University of Mississippi. That action was blasted by former board member Bobby Chain of Hattiesburg, who claimed that "a stacked board" dominated by Ole Miss and State had aborted the leadership plan without giving it a chance to work.[19]

The reassignment of the leadership role in journalism was part of a broader effort by the board to respond to the latest round of program reviews and to continue the process of eliminating marginal programs. Overall, the program reviews were discouraging and the board grappled with the decision of what programs to cut, keep, or consolidate. Of the 671 degree programs that had been reviewed, only 13 were commended; 514 were approved, 81 were given pending approval, 3 were given conditional approval, 59 were considered marginal, and one was to be phased out.[20]

In an editorial titled "Marginal, at Best," the *Jackson Daily News-The Clarion-Ledger* was generally critical of the state institutions of higher learning and challenged the board to make the hard decisions necessary to eliminate marginal programs and to concentrate the state's resources on developing a few areas of excellence. In responding to that rather disparaging editorial, the board explained that it had already eliminated several marginal programs and had upgraded others, and predicted that it might be forced to eliminate some good programs because of recent budget cuts.[21]

Several days after the board's gloomy response appeared in the Jackson press, the Mississippi legislature convened for the 1986 session. Among the most quarrelsome issues during that session was funding the public school system and the institutions of higher learning. The old rivalry between the common schools and higher education resurfaced on the eve of that session and some influential legislators agreed to push the public school bill during the first days of the session. Their strategy was successful and the school bill was passed. Higher education officials were displeased by that maneuver because there would be less money for higher education once the public school appropriation had been made. Their fears were not unfounded and both the junior colleges and the universities experienced deep cuts in their 1986-1987 appropriations. Those cuts were severe but they were not a surprise. They were only the latest of a series of cuts dating to 1981.[22]

Every fiscal year since 1981-82, except for 1984-85, the higher education budget had been reduced. In 1984, a special session of the legislature allocated a special appropriation to the College Board with a recommendation that the board study the feasibility of consolidating or closing some of the eight universities. And, following a norm that had been established many years earlier, the legislature authorized $100,000 for a study. The board accepted the legislature's suggestion and retained Jack D. Foster, head of a Kentucky educational consulting firm, to conduct the study. His report, known as the Foster Study, was published in January 1985.[23]

Closing MUW and Mississippi Valley State, according to the Foster Study, would not be as economical as it might seem because their students would likely transfer to other state schools and that would require expansion of those institutions. The state would also have to maintain the unused buildings at MUW and Mississippi Valley and pay off the bonded indebtedness on those buildings. Foster also studied the feasibility of consolidating some state institutions, but he was not enthusiastic about that option. The Foster Study found that public support for closing or consolidating institutions was in reality a call for retrenchment. "To some extent," Foster wrote, "we believe the call for closure or consolidation really is a call for the Board to take whatever action is necessary, however drastic it may be, to keep the cost of higher education within the financial means of the state."[24]

Like most previous studies, the Foster Study implored the board to take an active rather than a reactive role in the governance of higher education. One way the board could do that was to appoint a Commissioner of Higher Education and require university presidents to report to the board through the Commissioner rather than directly to the board. The Foster Study stated categorically that the autonomy of each institution must be surrendered in the interest of an overall state system of higher education. Finally, the Foster Study criticized the numerically driven funding formula and recommended that the board reexamine the basis of allocating funds to the eight universities.[25]

Another independent study of the funding formula conducted by Joseph E. Johnson validated the Foster Study's criticism of the funding process. The Johnson report that was issued on January 16, 1985 found that the existing formula, which the board had adopted in 1974, funded the "comprehensive universities less adequately than [the] regional universities" and recommended major revisions.[26]

The Board of Trustees in 1985 was sensitive to the criticism that its policies may have contributed to the financial crisis facing higher education, and in the spring of 1985, the board reviewed a wide range of options that would ameliorate the situation. At its March 1985 meeting, the board seriously considered consolidating Mississippi University for Women and Mississippi State. The board also considered closing Mississippi Valley and several off-campus centers. But after lengthy deliberations and discussions with alumni groups from Mississippi University for Women and Mississippi Valley, the board decided to maintain MUW "as a separate institution with its own mission." The board also voted to continue Mississippi Valley and adopted several measures to enhance the quality of education it provided. To stop the drain of funds from the parent campuses to branch campuses, the board directed that all off-campus centers, with three exceptions, become self supporting.[27]

Although the College Board did not have the constitutional or statutory authority to close a university, the board was blamed for the deepening financial crisis and public support for closing or consolidating some universities increased. Governor Bill Allain became one of the most vocal critics of the Board of Trustees and reiterated his claim that Mississippi could not support eight universities. The chairman of the house ways and means committee warned university presidents: "This business of having eight [universities] is gone. The only question is when."[28]

As the Board of Trustees prepared for its January 1986 meeting, it faced the prospects of major budget reductions, a governor who had criticized the board for not closing some of the universities, a sometimes hostile legislature, and an unsympathetic public. On the eve of their January meeting, several board members met with the legislative leadership. There was a lot of straight talk and the board left the meeting convinced that things were even worse than they had imagined.[29]

In the face of the funding crisis that showed no signs of abating in the immediate future, Chancellor R. Gerald Turner of the University of Mississippi acknowledged that "there must be some difficult decisions made" and expressed a willingness to accept those decisions. President Donald Zacharias of Mississippi State was even more emphatic. "If something dramatic is not done," he said, "something dramatic will happen by default." The recent budget cuts and the increasing likelihood that the formula would be revised in favor of the comprehensive universities had intensified the rivalry between the five regional universities and the big three. The presidents of the big three realized that many of the decisions dictated by current circumstances would be unpopular with the smaller schools and that institutional loyalties and rivalries could weaken the resolve of the Board of Trustees to make those hard decisions.[30]

Consequently, the university presidents, at the urging of Turner and Zacharias, called for a special, impartial, broadly based, statewide committee that would include legislators to study the funding formula and the general condition of higher education in Mississippi. On the basis of its study, the committee could "recommend long-range solutions--even program closures or consolidation--to avoid a repeat of the present financial crisis." The presidents of the comprehensive universities agreed to "follow the recommendations of an impartial committee made up of concerned Mississippi citizens, educators, and lawmakers." But the presidents of the regional universities, who stood to lose the advantage they had under the current funding formula, were skeptical that a truly objective study could be made. President James Strobel of Mississippi University for Women said he would be hesitant to endorse any study before it was conducted and saw little advantage in yet another study. "I've only been here nine years," he said, "and I have a roomful of studies."[31]

The fact that some presidents found it necessary and were willing to resort to a committee of concerned citizens revealed a structural flaw in the state's system of higher education: there were eight autonomous institutions, but there was not a commissioner of higher education with any degree of oversight of those institutions. Every study of higher education in Mississippi since 1925 had cited that flaw and had recommended a variety of ways to correct it. All of those studies agreed on two fundamentals. First, if the eight individual institutions of higher learning were to function as a coordinated state system of higher education, institutional autonomy would have to be surrendered. Second, if the Board of Trustees sought to function as a governing board rather than an administrative board, it had to remove itself from operational decisions by establishing an operational officer or Commissioner of Higher Education who would carry out the board's policies and decisions.

In the 1980s, the financial crisis forced the Board of Trustees to reexamine the tradition of institutional autonomy. And perhaps even more importantly, the retirement of Executive Secretary E. E. Thrash in August 1986 prompted the Board of Trustees to consider creating a Commissioner of Higher Education. Executive Secretary Thrash, whose distinguished, if sometime stormy, tenure dated to 1968, had long been a champion of institutional autonomy. Campus autonomy had also been supported by strong-willed board members of varying philosophical persuasions. But those trustees were no longer on the board and after Thrash's retirement, there were no determined advocates of autonomy on the board staff.

Shortly after Thrash announced his retirement, the Board of Trustees appointed a special committee to redefine and recast the role of the Executive Secretary. The committee recommended that the office of Executive Secretary be superseded by a Commissioner of Higher Education with broad authority and responsibility. The board accepted that recommendation and established the new office.

Following an extensive nationwide search, the Board of Trustees appointed William Ray Cleere as Mississippi's first Commissioner of Higher Education. At the time of his appointment in November 1987, Cleere was the vice-chancellor for academic affairs of the university system of Georgia. Although the Board of

Trustees drafted a job description outlining the powers and responsibilities of the new position, Commissioner Cleere in large measure defined the office as he exercised its authority. It was the intent of the board that the eight university presidents would report to the Board of Trustees through the Commissioner. However, the working relationship between the university presidents and the Commissioner of Higher Education was determined by the Commissioner's determination to exercise the authority of that office and the university presidents' deference to the office. While Commissioner Cleere was shaping the contours of his office, the Board of Trustees, in response to the *Ayers* lawsuit, was grappling with the traditional structure of Mississippi's system of higher education and the relationship between the state's eight universities.[32]

During the days of dissent following the Meredith Crisis, the African American community in Mississippi questioned the fairness of the allocation of state funds to the Historically Black Colleges and Universities. And in 1975, Jake Ayers, Sr. filed suit in federal court challenging the allocation process. After almost twenty years of legal wrangling, in 1992 a federal court ordered the state of Mississippi to rectify the years of discrimination against black college students. In response to that edict, the Board of Trustees recommended a major restructuring of Mississippi's system of state universities.

Under that new structure, Mississippi Valley students and faculty would be transferred to Cleveland and consolidated with Delta State into Delta Valley State University, which would be under the administrative control of the University of Mississippi. Alcorn State University would be administratively absorbed by Mississippi State, but would maintain its campus in Lorman. MUW would merge administratively with the University of Southern Mississippi at Hattiesburg, but would maintain its campus in Columbus. Jackson State University would be allocated several million dollars to expand and upgrade its curriculum and faculty to attract more white students. The plan would also close the College of Veterinary Medicine at Mississippi State and the School of Dentistry at the University of Mississippi Medical Center.

According to a College Board attorney, William Goodman, "This plan proposes four comprehensive, or level one, universities with shared missions and it would do away with the competition among state universities." Not unexpectedly, the plan "drew withering condemnation" from the African American community and the attorneys representing the *Ayers* plaintiffs. Alvin O. Chambliss Jr., lead attorney for the plaintiffs, said that "the winners may have lost." Mississippian William Raspberry, an African American and Pulitzer Prize-winning journalist with the Washington Post, expressed a common dilemma: "The consensus here is that the College Board hasn't figured out the right answer. I haven't either." The College Board's consolidation plan was abandoned under the weight of that "withering condemnation," and after several more years of adjudication, a settlement was finally reached in the spring of 2001. Under that settlement, the State of Mississippi agreed to appropriate $500 million to the HBCUs over a period of several years for academic programs and capital improvements.[33]

By the end of the twentieth century, Mississippi's eight public universities, in which the people invested so much of their precious resources, had not become the system of higher education that the people of Mississippi had hoped for since the founding of Jefferson College in 1802. But the search was not abandoned, and soon after the dawn of the new century, several bills were introduced in the legislature to restructure the system and the governance of higher education.

Footnotes Chapter 10

1 For McGuinness' quote, see Chapter Seven, "The States and Higher Education," in Philip G. Altbach, Robert O. Berdhal, and Patricia J. Gumport, (eds.), *American Higher Education in the Twenty-First Century: Social, Political, and Economic Challenges* (2005), 198; see also Robert Berdhal, *Statewide Coordination of Higher Education* (1971); Hugh Davis Graham, "Structure and Governance of Higher Education: Historical and Comparative Analysis in State Policy," *Journal of Policy History* (1989) I, 80-107; John D. Millett, *Conflict in Higher Education, State Government Versus Institutional Independence* (1984).

2 *Clarion-Ledger*, April 16, 1974; *Jackson Daily News*, April 19, 1974; *Commercial Appeal*, April 19, 1974.

3 Eugene W. Hickok, Jr., "Higher Education, the State, and the Politics of Administration in Mississippi," (Ph. D diss., University of Virginia, 1983), 10.

4 *Jackson Daily News*, February 15, 1974; interview with Governor William L. Waller on February 29, 1979 in Jackson, Mississippi; see Bill Waller, *Straight Ahead, The Memoirs of a Mississippi Governor* (2007), Chapter 13, "Education–The Highest Priority," 155-172.

5 *Clarion-Ledger*, October 2, 1974.

6 Undated clipping from the *Reflector* in the Holmes Collection.

7 *Student Printz*, March 15, 1977.

8 Interviews with Verner Smith Holmes and Euclid R. Jobe; *Minutes*, January 17, 1980

9 *Minutes*, April 19, December 20, 1973.

10 *Clarion-Ledger*, February 20, 1975; *Daily Corinthian*, June 19, 1974.

11 *Minutes*, August 21, 1975; *Clarion-Ledger*, September 16, 1975.

12 *Minutes*, January 15, 1976; *Jackson Daily News*, January 15, 1976; *Oxford Eagle*, January 16, 1976; *Daily Journal*, January 27, 1976.

13 *Minutes*, July 15, 1976.

14 *Minutes*, March 15, 1979.

15 The Academy for Educational Development, Inc., *Program Review: A Structure for Mississippi's Public Universities* (1979), Introduction, 1-3.

16 *Minutes,* November 18, 1981; a copy of the mission statements and the "Official Explanation," dated March 21, 1982, are in the Holmes Collection.

17 Ibid.

18 Board of Trustees, "Centers of Excellence;" a copy of this document along with a letter explaining the rationale for centers of excellence from Executive Secretary Thrash to Senator John T. Fraiser, Jr., chairman of the senate appropriations committee, dated February 2, 1983, is in the Holmes Collection.

19 *Daily Journal,* July 20, August 16, 1984; *Daily Mississippian,* July 26, 1984; see also Bobby Chain, *Bobby Lee Chain, The Life and Journals of a Mississippi Entrepreneur* (2010).

20 See detailed article by Andy Kanengiser in *Jackson Daily News-The Clarion-Ledger,* January 5, 1986.

21 Denton Rogers to Robert Gordon, January 19, 1986, a copy of this letter is in the Holmes Collection.

22 Interview with Representative Glenn Endris and Representative Ed Perry on February 26, 1986 in Jackson, Mississippi.

23 Board of Trustees, "Appropriations and Reductions 1981-82 through 1985-86," a copy of this document is in the Holmes Collection; see also Jack D. Foster, *Restructuring Higher Education: Choices and Analysis for Mississippi* (1985).

24 Foster, *Restructuring Higher Education,* 60-63.

25 Ibid, 54-57, 70-72.

26 Joseph E. Johnson, *Review of Funding and Allocation Formula* (1985), 2.

27 *Minutes,* March 14, 1985.

28 *Clarion-Ledger,* March 6, 1986.

29 Interview with Representatives Glenn Endris and Ed Perry.

30 *Clarion-Ledger,* February 2, March 5, 24, 1986; interview with Chancellor R. Gerald Turner on February 20, 1989 at the University of Mississippi.

31 *Clarion-Ledger,* August 21, 1986; interview with Will Hickman, Board of Trustees, on February 29, 1989 at Oxford Mississippi.

32 This information was obtained in several interviews with Commissioner Cleere.

33 For the details of the College Board's recommendation in response to the *Ayers* suit, see *Minutes,* October 19-20, 1992; see also *New York Times,* October 23, 1992; *Washington Post,* December 7, 1992; Cliff E. Williams, *The Ayers Case* (2005?); for the 2001 agreement, see Google search Ayers Settlement Agreement Mississippi Board of Trustees; see also *Clarion-Ledger,* January 10, 2015.

Chapter 11
Restructuring the Governance of Higher Education, 2000-2015

Higher Education is a Troubled Giant.

John Thelin

The twenty-first century did not begin well for Mississippi's Troubled Giant. In the spring of 2000, Mississippi's slumping economy forced deep cuts in the budgets of Mississippi's institutions of higher learning. Budget cuts require tough decisions, and tough decisions prompt complaints. In 2001, two college presidents were embroiled in controversy that led to the dismissal of one and the resignation of the other. One college president survived a determined effort to remove him, and a fourth president resigned after only two years and took a higher paying job in Alabama.[1]

In early February 2001, a rally of about two hundred Alcorn alumni on the Lorman campus repeated their previous but more private demand that the football coach be dismissed after an 0-11 season, which followed two losing seasons. But students among that crowd added, "We have more issues than just a football team." Two politically influential alumni who spoke at the rally included State Representatives Alyce Clarke of Jackson and Phillip West of Natchez. One prominent alumnus said, "We're not trying to run the institution, but we are saying that what we have now is not working."

Some prominent Alcorn alumni accused the College Board of turning "deaf ears to their complaints about ASU President Clinton Bristow." A Jackson alumnus who wanted "Bristow removed from his post," complained that "you can't get past" the Commissioner of Higher Education. After an initial meeting, he said, the Commissioner "has refused two requests by the alumni to meet again." Several months after that rally on the campus, the *Clarion-Ledger* reported "another movement of disgruntled Alcorn alumni to remove the president." The Board of Trustees did not respond to those disgruntled alumni, and President Bristow, who was also highly regarded by many alumni, weathered that troubled summer and remained president until his untimely death five years later.[2]

The Board of Trustees was scheduled to review the contract of University of Southern Mississippi President Horace Fleming in June 2001, but his review was

141

postponed as the trustees were dealing with the impending resignation of MUW President Clyda Rent, who had been under fire from her faculty for more than two years. Dr. Rent, a highly regarded academic sociologist, was appointed president of MUW in 1989. Since its founding in 1884, the "woman's college" had never had a woman president. President Rent's appointment was hailed as the beginning of a new era in the history of the first public woman's college in the United States. Under her leadership, MUW won recognition as an outstanding liberal arts college and for several years, *U.S. News and World Report* named it the No.1 public Southern Regional liberal arts college. During her first decade, the W's enrollment more than doubled and she was instrumental in preventing its closure or consolidation.

But all was not well at the woman's college. As she entered the tenth year of her twelve year administration, the lingering contention between President Rent and her faculty found an angry and public expression in a vote of no confidence. In August 1999, MUW's one-hundred and forty faculty members, by a 70% majority, adopted a vote of no confidence. The contention between the president and the professors, according to the faculty, was caused by her micromanagement and a lack of communication.

The Board of Trustees instructed Commissioner Tom Layzell to confer with the faculty and the president and resolve the issues if possible. But the issues and ill will that had been brewing for several years were not abated, and at the board meeting in June 2001, following a seven hour closed session, President Rent resigned. She was named President Emeritus and joined her husband as a member of the faculty at Mississippi State University.[3]

In that long, hot summer of 2001, as the contract of President Horace Fleming was coming up for renewal, "rumors surfaced that some USM alumni, in particular supporters of the athletic program, were bombarding the board with faxes and telephone calls requesting Fleming's removal." But some alumni and students rallied to his defense. One professor compared his eventual dismissal to "a hanging on the square."

Inaugurated in 1997, President Fleming had chosen not to exercise an option authorized by the Board of Trustees to raise student fees in support of athletics. His adamant support for the expansion of the USM Gulf Coast campus also prompted some opposition from board members who protected the interests of Mississippi State and Ole Miss. In January 2001, as a financial crisis loomed, the Board of Trustees authorized university presidents to eliminate some academic programs and faculty positions. But President Fleming "criticized the idea openly," and announced, "I am not going to whistle past the graveyard." A month later, the College Board directed President Fleming to reduce expenditures for the current year.

To offset the ramifications of that cutback, the University of Southern Mississippi's fundraising apparatus kicked into high gear. But an influential athletics fund raiser made light of the University's fundraising prospects: "It seems that the only thing they are good at is going to meetings and drinking designer water and eating boiled shrimp that somebody else peeled." Former president of the Board of Trustees, Bobby Chain, acknowledged but dismissed the claim that opposition to President Fleming was about athletics. "I like Horace Fleming," he said, "but this is deeper than athletics." The rapid turnover of administrative personnel and what the *Hattiesburg American* called "unpresidential criticism" of the Board of Trustees figured prominently into the nonrenewal of President Fleming's contract. The president of the College Board regretted the publicity surrounding the contract renewal and said, "When it gets in the paper, it doesn't help the institution, the president, or the board."

After a five hour closed meeting on July 19, 2001, the Board of Trustees voted 11-1 not to renew President Fleming's contract, but did offer him a one year extension, which he declined. After his tenure at Southern ended, the Board of Trustees retained him as a consultant for one year at a salary of $134,000. A faculty member scorned the Board's action: "The behavior of the Board is an embarrassment; they acted like a bush league operation. He wasn't good enough to be president, but a 'consultant.' Sounds more like alimony in a divorce case." Whatever the trustees may have done to bring down upon themselves such ignominy, they quickly wove their way back into the good graces of Southern alumni by naming former USM president Aubrey Lucas interim president.[4]

In an August 17, 2001 editorial under the heading, "State's College Presidents Becoming Easy Targets," the *Clarksdale Press Register* reviewed the recent shakeup of college presidents and excoriated the Board of Trustees: "Enough is enough. The College Board must send a strong message that it is guided by the best interest of its member institutions, not the whims of faculty and alumni snivelers."

Six months after that editorial, the Mississippi legislature convened and within days, the lawmakers were discussing the "whims of faculty and alumni," debating the structure of the governance of higher education, and introducing bills left and right. In the 2002 legislative session, twenty-one bills and resolutions were introduced to restructure, modify, or reconstitute the governance of higher education. The issue was not if, but how, the governance of higher education would be restructured.

One resolution would abolish the existing governing board and replace it with a separate board for each institution.

Another would reduce the twelve year terms to eight years, and another would match the term of board members with the term of the governors who appointed them.

Another resolution would merge all of the Mississippi boards of education into one central board that would govern education from kindergarten through graduate school.

HCR 69 would reconstitute the board with four members appointed from each of the three supreme court districts, and include an alumnus from each institution.

HB1245 would require that the "Big 4" play each other in football.

None of these bills or resolutions were enacted.

But the legislature did enact Senate Concurrent Resolution 522 after it was significantly amended in the House of Representatives. SCR 522 authorized a constitutional amendment that would restructure the Board of Trustees of State Institutions of Higher Learning. The amendment was placed on the ballot in the general election of November 4, 2003 and approved by an 85% majority. An 85% percent approval of a candidate, a bill, a referendum, or a constitutional amendment is a rare spectacle in Mississippi. And in a strange sort of way, that 85% may not have been so much an expression of unanimity, as an expression of discontent with the way the universities were being governed.[5]

Mississippi was not the only state that modified its governing structure in 2004. The Association of Governing Boards of Universities and Colleges published a forty-one page document, *State Governance Action Annual 2004, Balancing Act: Public Higher Education in Transition*, in which it reviewed the restructuring of the governance of higher education in twenty-three states.

The constitutional amendment implemented in 2004 established a twelve-member Board of Trustees appointed by the governor with the consent of the senate. Four trustees were appointed from each of the three supreme court districts to nine year staggered terms, with four new board members appointed every four years. The tradition of staggered terms is predicated on an old and enduring consensus that one governor should not control the Board of Trustees of Institutions of Higher Learning. In a 2011 interview with one of the authors of SCR 522, journalist Bobby Harrison asked him if the legislature had taken into account the fact that since governors could succeed themselves, one governor could make all twelve appointments to the College Board. "It was all happenstance," the senator explained, "I don't think anybody was looking ahead to see who would be governor" when the change was made. He went on to explain that the governing structure was changed because the appointment of board members from the congressional districts as they existed in the 1940s did not reflect recent population shifts and second, many legislators thought twelve year terms were too long.[6]

The goal or aim or purpose of the 2004 restructuring of the governance of higher education was not clearly defined or identified by those who introduced SCR 522, except to shorten the terms and to make the board's membership more reflective of recent population shifts. The restructured board did not reduce the rivalry among the eight universities for the state's meager resources or shield the university presidents from angry public discourse. Nor did it shield the universities from the recurring demands for closure or merger.

In the fall of 2009, Governor Haley Barbour recommended the merger of Alcorn State and Valley State with Jackson State. Governor Barbour said the merger was necessary because of growing budget constraints. Mergers, he added, would be preferable to closures. The College Board reacted quickly to the governor's recommendation and announced that it would reduce spending at all eight universities, and would consider the governor's recommendation.

Matt Thomas, a prescient Alcorn State alumnus, predicted that "Alcorn State and Valley State will merge with Jackson State the day after Mississippi State and the University of Southern Mississippi merge with Ole Miss." Governor Barbour's proposal to merge the HBCUs was dead on arrival.[7]

Governor Barbour also recommended the consolidation of MUW with Mississippi State. But MUW faculty, students, and alumni had something else to worry about. President Claudia Limbert was trying to change the name of the "woman's college" that had become coeducational in 1982. In an April 26, 2009 article in the Columbus *Dispatch*, President Limbert explained the reason for her recommendation: "Our name was an issue when we went co-ed 27 years ago and was a topic upon my arrival at MUW [in 2002] when a new study indicated the University had a serious identify crisis.... Those who say we can grow significantly with our current name cannot rebut the evidence that only 3 percent of women nationally say they would consider a women's college, which is how we are perceived because of our name. This fact explains why in 1960 there were more than 300 women's colleges and today there are less than 60."

President Limbert's recommendation ignited a furor and an ugly response from the Alumnae Association, which still used the feminine spelling for the term alumni. Her name change also incurred the wrath of one alumnus. In an August 23, 2009 letter to the editor of the *Delta Democrat Times*, an alumnus wrote that President Limbert's claim "that men are embarrassed to call themselves W graduates gives me and my fellow W guys no credit for enlightenment, intelligence, or common sense. W guys go there for the same reasons W girls go there: smaller classes…quality programs…and the chance to be active in organizations, publications and student government." He also criticized her for "the demise of the athletic program" and for "the divisive act of cutting ties with the alumnae association (of which I am a member of the board of directors) and trying to create a new one." After a prolonged and unseemly row with the Alumnae Association, President Limbert disassociated MUW from its original alumnae association and established a new alumni association. The Alumnae Association filed suit against President Limbert, but the Mississippi State Supreme Court ruled in favor of President Limbert.

President Limbert's tenure was also tainted by an issue of academic freedom involving a professor who was removed as head of the Division of Science and Mathematics after lecturing on the "flaws in the Darwinian theory [and presenting] alternative views to evolution such as intelligent design." The professor's removal "received national media exposure" and prompted "more than 500 e-mails" to the Board of Trustees demanding her reinstatement. President Limbert reinstated the professor to her position.

The ugly and prolonged discourse between President Limbert and her detractors ended in the fall of 2009 when she announced that she would not seek reappointment when her contract expired June 30, 2010. With her resignation, the push for a name change also ended.[8]

President Claudia Limbert's tenure at Mississippi University for Women provides a case study of the timorous sojourn of a president at an institution of higher learning in Mississippi. Upon the announcement of her appointment as the university's thirteenth president in 2002, one prominent alumna said it was "an easy decision because of the many qualities Limbert brings." Two other prominent alumnae said, "We're thrilled, she's the perfect match," and "she's the perfect fit for us." In reference to President Limbert a female member of the Board of Trustees said, "Every now and then you get the perfect person at the right time." Some of those very alumnae would later become President Limbert's severest critics, and would take her to court.[9]

President Limbert's troubled tenure was replicated in various forms and degrees at other Mississippi institutions of higher learning and validated John Thelin's depiction of higher education as a troubled giant.

On March 27, 2006, the College Board announced that four star general Robert H. Fogelsong was the unanimous choice for president at Mississippi State. Two years later, the headlines of the March 13, 2008 *Stars and Stripes* read: "Former USAFE Boss Quits Post as Complaints Mount." The opening sentence read, "Retired Air Force General Robert 'Doc' Fogelsong quit as president of Mississippi State University this week amid gripes from students and faculty over everything from the removal of campus daffodils to his micromanaging leadership style." The

Chapter 11 — Restructuring the Goverance of Higher Education, 2000-2015

opening sentence in the *Clarion-Ledger* article on March 8, 2008 announcing his resignation read: "For the third time in ten years, Mississippi State University is looking for a new president."

After President Fogelsong resigned, the College Board unanimously appointed Vance Watson, the popular vice-president of the Division of Agriculture, interim president. There was speculation that Watson would be named president of Mississippi State University. However, after the media reported that Interim President Watson had allowed Mississippi State personnel to landscape Higher Education Commissioner Tom Meredith's lawn at his Rankin County home, he was forced to resign and was no longer considered for the president's position. On October 20, 2008, *The Chronicle of Higher Education* reported that, following a "landscaping scandal," Commissioner Meredith retired.

In 2008, Mississippi Valley State University was also in the process of a presidential search. Interim President Roy Hudson, who had a long and distinguished career at Valley State, was the favorite of the faculty and the Legislative Black Caucus. When the College Board did not appoint Hudson, an October 15, 2008 article in the *Clarion-Ledger* quoted State Senator David Jordan, a Valley alumnus from Greenwood, who said "We all had endorsed and supported [Dr. Roy Hudson], and we are concerned about why he was passed over. We don't understand that." During Hudson's tenure as interim president, an administrative assistant had misused some Mississippi Valley Foundation funds, but Hudson was not personally accused of any malfeasance.

The Watson/Meredith issue and the controversy over the presidential appointment at Mississippi Valley State in 2008 led to a board policy stipulating that interim presidents would not be eligible for appointment as president.

Things were just as tumultuous at the University of Southern Mississippi. After the nonrenewal of President Fleming's contract in 2002, the Board of Trustees named Shelby Thames, a world renowned polymer scientist, the eighth president of USM. President Thames was a strong proponent of "university-industry collaboration that began over three decades earlier with the creation of the polymer science program." Several members of the liberal arts faculty were suspicious of President Thames' academic priorities. The College Board elected Thames president of USM by a vote of 11-1. The lone vote in opposition to his appointment was cast by a graduate of USM, who said, "This is a very fractured university." In the previous decade or so, the University of Southern Mississippi had lost ground in its continuing bid to keep up with State and Ole Miss, and some alumni hoped that under President Thames, their alma mater could regain some of that lost ground. But a survey by the local chapter of the American Association of University Professors indicated that 85% of the USM faculty opposed Thames' appointment. "I hope it all works out well," said the Southern graduate on the Board of Trustees, "I literally put my heart and soul into this search." Unfortunately, it did not work out well. An inaccurate, but probably unintentional, student enrollment report exaggerated USM's enrollment and severely damaged the institution's credibility. On April 5, 2004, the *Mississippi Business Journal* reported that the summary dismissal of two tenured faculty members, who were also locked out of their offices, had attracted national and international attention. The two professors had challenged the accuracy of President Thames' new vice-president's academic credentials, which they said were embellished.

The dismissal of the two faculty members "brought to a boiling point conflicts that [had] simmered" since President Thames' appointment. USM Professor William Scarborough, one of America's premier historians, said the dismissals "were the last straw" and added, "I think we need to petition the board of trustees to terminate Shelby Thames immediately." Here were two men of great ability and high self esteem, President Thames and Professor Scarborough, at loggerheads, which is not uncommon on college campuses. It was inevitable that the College Board would be drawn into the fray. One board member derided the critics of President Thames as "a lynch mob." The situation was eventually resolved. The two dismissed faculty members were not reinstated, but were offered two year contracts after which they would not be renewed. And the College Board approved President Thames' request that "he remain at his post for two more years," after which he would return "to my first love–the lab." He was given another one year extension and remained in office until 2007. But the trouble at Southern Miss was not over yet.[10]

As the search for a successor to President Thames was beginning, the University of Southern Mississippi Alumni Association established a fifteen member presidential transition team. The alumni "acknowledged the college board's authority to make the final choice," but they also acknowledged the alumni's "large stake in the outcome of the presidential search and, therefore, have chosen to provide a forum for dialogue, discussion, research, and resolution." The USM alumni president said, "Controlling our own destiny is an absolute must."

On May 21, 2007, the Board of Trustees appointed a Southern alumna, Martha Dunagin Saunders, president of the University of Southern Mississippi. She was the Chancellor of University of Wisconsin-Whitewater, and was the first woman president of one of Mississippi's three comprehensive universities. She had a BA in French from Southern, an MA in journalism from the University of Georgia, and a Ph. D in communication theory from Florida State. According to Chester Morgan, historian of the University of Southern Mississippi, "It was in many ways an inspired choice." But five years later, unexpectedly, President Saunders resigned for "personal reasons." After her resignation she said, "What I will miss least, is not having any control over my life. . . . College presidents are on the job 24-7."[11]

After President Saunders' resignation the College Board appointed Dr. Rodney D. Bennett president of the University of Southern Mississippi. Dr. Bennett was the tenth president of USM, and the first African American president of a traditionally white institution of higher learning in Mississippi.

When Dr. Donna H. Oliver was appointed the sixth president of Mississippi Valley State University in 2009, she also made history as the first woman president of an HBCU in Mississippi. She succeeded President Lester Newman, who resigned in 2007 under pressure from the faculty and alumni. Two years after her inauguration, President Oliver was given a vote of no confidence by the Mississippi Valley faculty senate, and in October 2012, the Board of Trustees voted not to renew her contract. When her successor, Dr. William B. Bynum, Jr. was appointed in 2013, Roosevelt Yarbrough, the president of the Mississippi Valley alumni association, expressed reservations about President Bynum, not because he was unqualified, but because he was not an alumnus of Mississippi Valley.[12]

However, even the appointment of an alumnus does not foretell a tranquil tenure. Few events in Mississippi's troubled history of higher education have provoked such a deep and wide response as did the College Board's decision to allow the contract of Chancellor Dan Jones to expire. On March 20, 2015 the Board of Trustees voted 9-2 to begin a search for a new chancellor, which, in effect, was a nonrenewal of Chancellor Jones' contract. Jones was a graduate of The University of Mississippi Medical Center, and before his appointment as chancellor in 2009, he had served as Vice-Chancellor for Health Affairs and Dean of the School of Medicine since 2003. During his tenure as Vice-Chancellor for Health Affairs, and as Chancellor of The University of Mississippi, both institutions experienced significant growth and expansion. The general public was shocked by the nonrenewal of Jones' contract. The basic issue that led to the nonrenewal of his contract was the governance of The University of Mississippi Medical Center. After Jones' nonrenewal became a public issue and many prominent Ole Miss alumni had demanded his reinstatement, the College Board offered him a two year contract, which he declined. Following his tenure as chancellor, Jones will hold the Sanderson Chair in Obesity, Metabolic Diseases, and Nutrition Research at the Medical Center.[13]

Adding to the public's dismay over the nonrenewal of Jones' contract was the flurry surrounding the Commissioner of Higher Education position. In January 2015, Commissioner Hank Bounds resigned as Commissioner of Higher Education to become President of the University of Nebraska. In February, the Board of

Trustees, without a formal search, appointed the popular and highly regarded Jim Borsig, the president of MUW, Commissioner of Higher Education. In March, the Board of Trustees voted to begin a search for a chancellor of The University of Mississippi. During the furor that decision incited, Borsig's appointment was greeted with a measure of relief, but not for long. In the weeks after his appointment, Borsig and Jones, with mutual respect, discussed the board's offer to extend Jones' contract for two years. On April 2, 2015, Jones declined the two year extension. Seven days later, Borsig announced that he would return as President of MUW. Eight days later, the Board of Trustees, without a formal search, elevated Associate Commissioner of Higher Education Dr. Glenn Boyce to the office of Commissioner of Higher Education.

This turmoil occurred while the legislature was in session and according to an old saying, "no one is safe when the legislature is in session." In the House of Representatives, sixty-nine members signed a letter in support of Chancellor Jones and as Bobby Harrison of the *Daily Journal* reported, "There has even been conversations in some circles of tying funding for the institutions of higher learning to the Jones decision." Representative Brad Mayo of Oxford recommended a study of the "higher education governing structures in other states" and the possibility of modifying the governing system in Mississippi. In the upper house, forty senators joined Senator Gray Tollison of Oxford in authoring a resolution to restructure the governance of higher education by establishing a central board with authority over the university system, and a separate governing board for each of the eight universities. These bills were introduced near the end of the session and no action was taken.[14]

There are those in the legislature and in the general public who believe Mississippi's system of governance should be changed because of the troubled tenures of several university presidents who were terminated or resigned amid ugly controversies. However, there have been many university presidents who served long and rather tranquil tenures under this same system of governance. John White was president of Mississippi Valley for twenty-one years. Walter Washington was president at Alcorn for twenty-five years. Kent Wyatt served twenty-four years as president of Delta State. In a period of forty-one years, there were only two presidents at the University of Southern Mississippi, William D. McCain and Aubrey Lucas. At Mississippi State University, President William Giles served ten years and Donald Zacharias served twelve years. At Ole Miss, Chancellor J. D. Williams served twenty-two years, Porter Fortune served sixteen years, Gerald Turner served eleven years, and Robert Khayat served fourteen years. The average tenure of a college president in the United States in 2011 was seven years, which was down from eight and a half years in 2006.[15]

Observations

Governing the troubled giant in the twentieth-first century is a convoluted process because modern American universities, unlike Old Time Colleges, are dynamic institutions in constant motion. Historians Robert Birnbaum and Peter D. Eckel characterize institutions of higher learning as "organized anarchies." In a world of ravishing changes, alumni are overly protective of their alma maters, who sheltered them in their youth. According to Christopher J. Lucas, the governance of higher education has also been complicated by the fact that a university is now "a corporate enterprise...congruent in all major respects with free-enterprise-capitalism [and] adept at marketing themselves [by] adapting curricular offerings to changes or shifts in market demand." Universities are a local industry, and presidents are commonly referred to as the CEO.

Consequently, chambers of commerce, local politicians, legislators, alumni, athletic associations, accrediting agencies, the student body and the faculty senate, boards of trustees, and presidents all share in the governance of higher education. In their massive study of American academia, Jack Schuster and Martin Finkelstein have found that "almost no one is pleased with the way campuses are governed: not the faculty, not administrators, not governing boards."[16]

Perhaps it is time to modify Mississippi's governing structure, especially in regard to the appointment process. There seems to be widespread agreement that one governor should not appoint the entire governing board. Geographic distribution of board membership is perhaps a relic of yesterday, and some consideration might be given to a modification of the appointing authority. Perhaps the Governor, Lieutenant Governor, and the Speaker of the House should be authorized to make appointments to the College Board. Faculty members and students have a stake in the governance of higher education, and they should have some voice in its governance, as they do in several states.

In the fifty states, there are two basic types of governing boards. In type one, there is a central board that governs the colleges and universities that comprise the state's system of higher education. Some central boards govern both junior and senior colleges, but in some states, like Mississippi, there are separate boards that govern the junior and senior colleges. The second type of governance includes one or more overall boards of trustees with limited authority that oversee the state system of higher education, but each college or university in the system has its own governing board. At latest count, there are twenty-three states that employ the central governing board, and twenty-four states that employ the institutional governing boards. Three states use some combination of the two systems.

The Education Commission of the States provides a data base that explains in some detail the various governing structures employed in each of the fifty states.[17]

The Mississippi legislature, with an advisory commission composed of Mississippians, is competent to study the governance of higher education and to make the changes that will allow Mississippi's governing board or boards to guard the interests of our institutions and protect the future of our children. If the troubled history of higher education tells us anything, it tells us that there is no system of governance that can place the institutions of higher learning above or beyond the mischief of politics or personalities.

It will do us all well to realize, and to remember, that it is not the system of governance, but the governors of the system, that make it work.

Footnotes Chapter 11

1 For the John R. Thelin quote, see *A History of American Higher Education* (2010), 316, which he allowed me to slightly modify in a telephone conversation on June 9, 2015; see also Amy E. Wells Dolan, Chapter 14, "The Challenge of Writing The South," 187-199 in Marybeth Gasman, [ed.], *The History of U.S. Higher Education, Methods of Understanding the Past* (2010).

2 On the Alcorn University situation, see *Vicksburg Post*, February 5, July 27, 2001; *Natchez Democrat*, August 17, 2001.

3 On Clyda Rent's tenure and resignation, see *Daily Journal*, September 19, 1997; June 23, 2001.

4 For a discussion of the nonrenewal of President Fleming's contract, see Chester M. Morgan, *Treasured Past, Golden Future: The Centennial History of the University of Southern Mississippi* (2010), 228-237.

5 Copies of these bills and resolutions can be found on the Mississippi Legislature Home Page at http://www.legislature.ms.gov/Pages/default.aspx; *Mississippi Official and Statistical Register 2004-2008*, 658-659; the MOSR is also called *The Blue Book*.

6 For Harrison's interview with the senator, see http://blog.gulflive.com/mississippi-press-news/2011/11/gov-elect_bryants_8_appointmen.html

7 For Governor Barbour's proposal, see *clarionledger.com* November 17, 2009; see also http://archive.thedmonline.com/article/miss-university-leaders-react-barbour; for Thomas' statement, see the HBCU blog, "JSU Prez stands by his HBCU merger plan," February 1, 2010.

8 *Clarion-Ledger*, March 15, 2003.; Columbus *Dispatch*, October 12, 2009.

9 These laudatory descriptions of President Limbert are quoted in the *Daily Journal*, April 6, 2002.

10 The complexities surrounding the tenure of President Shelby Thames and the dissension among his faculty are discussed by Morgan, *Treasured Past, Golden Future*, 241-272; 277-287.

11 For President Saunders' tenure, see USM News Release April 5, 2007; and on her resignation see various Google searches, specifically "USM President Martha Saunders Resigns Suddenly."

12 On the tenure of President Oliver, see Google searches, "History-making Oliver Forges Ahead Under Blurry Conditions;" "Faculty Senate Votes 'No Confidence' in President of Mississippi Valley State University;" and "No Contract Renewal for MVSU President."

13 For numerous articles on his nonrenewal, see various Google searches on Chancellor Dan Jones and The University of Mississippi; see especially Clay Chandler and Jerry Mitchell, "IHL Offers Few Words, Little Clarity After Meeting," *Clarion-Ledger* website, March 27, 2015; and Sam R. Hall, "What Went Down With Dan Jones, College Board," *Clarion-Ledger* website, April 4, 2015.

14 There are many newspaper and journal articles detailing these events that may be found on Google searches; see Bobby Harrison, "Tollison Proposes IHL Overhaul, Separate Boards for Universities," *Daily Journal*, website, March 25, 2015; see Senate Concurrent Resolution 654, Mississippi Legislature 2015 Regular Session; IHL Press Release, April 17, 2015; Jeff Amy, "College Board Defends System," Associated Press website, April 19, 2015.

15 For the average tenure of college presidents, see the Association of Governing Boards of Universities and Colleges website, "What is the Average Tenure of a College or University President"

16 For the "organized anarchies" quote, see Robert Birnbaum and Peter D. Eckel, Chapter Twelve, "The Dilemma of Presidential Leadership," 340-365 in Altbach, et. al. [eds.], *American Higher Education*; Christopher J. Lucas, *American Higher Education, A History* (2006), 257-260; for the last quote, see Jack H. Schuster and Martin J. Finkelstein, *The American Faculty: The Restructuring of Academic Work and Careers* (2006), 358.

17 On the governing systems employed in the fifty states, see Aims C. McGuinness, Jr. Chapter Seven, "The States and Higher Education," 198-225, in Altbach, et. al. [eds.], *American Higher Education*; see also the Education Commission of the States website, "Postsecondary Governance: Online Database," at www.ecs.org/clearinghouse/31/02/3102.htm; and see also Association of Governing Boards of Universities and Colleges, *The 2014 Survey of Higher Education Governance*.

Index

A

Academy for Educational Development 132, 139
Alcorn Agricultural and Mechanical College 19, 36, 38, 101, 118
  Alcorn A&M 38-41, 46, 47, 52, 59, 69, 77, 82
  see also Alcorn State University
Alcorn State University 16, 19, 37, 38, 93, 94, 96, 97, 99, 104, 119, 120, 133, 138, 141, 145, 150, 152
  see also Alcorn Agricultural and Mechanical College
Alcorn, James L. 34, 35, 37
Allain, Bill 136
American Association of State Universities 73
American Pharmaceutical Association 73
Ames, Adelbert 37, 38, 47
Angell, James B. 33
Ayers, Jake 138, 140
Ayers lawsuit 138, 140

B

Bailey, Thomas 87, 91
Baker, Bill 8, 55, 60
Barbour, Haley 145, 152
Barnard, Frederick A. P. 22, 28-31, 35
Barnett, Ross 100, 101, 104-115, 124
Barrett, Russell 101, 104, 113, 114, 118
Barton, Bill 100
Bass, Jack 113, 123
Belhaven 43
Bell, William H. 93, 101
Bennett, Claude 67, 69, 79
Bennett, Rodney D. 149
Bilbo, Theodore G. 23, 54-57, 59-80, 83, 88, 91
Birnbaum, Robert 151, 153
Black, Hugo 104
Blount, Katie 8

Blue Mountain 43
Board of Trustees 8, 11, 12, 14, 15, 18, 19, 23-31, 34-43, 45-47, 49-54, 56, 57, 60, 62, 65-71, 73, 75, 77-87, 89, 91-94, 96-101, 105-108, 113-124, 128-138, 140-144, 146-150
Bond, Nathaniel 71
Bond, Willard F. 57, 75
Borne, Ron 8, 113
Borsig, Jim 150
Bounds, Hank 149
Bowdre, Paul 70
Bowen, David 118
Boyce, Glenn 150
Brandon, Gerard C. 13
Bridgforth, Lucie Robertson 72, 76, 101, 125
Brister, Milton 129
Bristow, Clinton 141
Brookings Study 74, 77, 78
Brown Decision 1954 7, 98
Brown, Albert G. 21-24, 30
Brunini, Ed 107, 110
Bryan, Harry 57
Bryan, William Jennings 44
Burgin, Bill 85, 88
Burkitt, Frank 33, 40, 45, 50, 53
Butler, Carl 118
Butts, Alfred 70, 94
Bynum, William B. 149

C

Carpenter, Corrine T. 118
Carter, Hodding 96
Centenary College 15, 18, 19
Centers of Academic Excellence 133
Chain, Bobby 134, 140, 143
Chamberlain, Duncan H. 51
Chamberlain, Jeremiah 15-17, 19
Chambliss Jr., Alvin O. 138
Citizens' Council 107, 125
Claiborne, W. C. C. 10, 17
Clap, Thomas 9, 17
Clarke, Alyce 141
Clark, Walter 54
Cleere, William Ray 137, 138, 140
Closed Society 22, 97, 99, 103, 113, 117, 124, 125, 129

Coleman, James P. 8, 101, 111, 113, 114
College Board 8, 12, 15, 46, 61, 69, 84, 87,
    89, 91, 93, 94, 96, 97, 99, 104, 108,
    115, 118, 123, 124, 128-130, 135,
    136, 138-149, 151, 152
Colvard, Dean W. 116, 125
Commissioner of Higher Education 58,
    68, 78, 80, 135, 137, 138, 141, 149,
    150
Committee of One Hundred 57
Conner, Martin Sennett 60, 77, 79, 85
Conner, Mike 55
Cook, Joseph Anderson 57, 60, 66, 67, 77,
    79, 85
Cook, Robert C. 95, 96, 101
cow college 44
Crawley, David E. 77, 86
Crider, Joseph 72
Critz, Hugh 70, 79

D

Davis, Jefferson 30, 31
Davis, Russell 121, 122
Delta State University 75, 77, 91, 96, 100,
    133, 138, 150
    Delta State College 100
    Delta State Teachers College 52,
        69, 81, 91, 93, 100
    Delta Valley State University 138
Doar, John 109, 110
Dolan, Amy Wells 8, 152
Dorman, Clarence 92
Dubra, Charles 97, 98, 103

E

Eagles, Charles 113, 114
Eaton, Clement 14, 17, 19
Eckel, Peter D. 151, 153
Elizabeth Female Academy 12, 18
Ellard, J. A. 91
Ellis, William A. 53
Emmerich, Oliver 86, 91, 100, 122
eternal vigilance 94, 131
Evers, Charles 119-121
Evers, Medgar 98, 101

Executive Secretary 78, 79, 81, 83, 85, 91,
    103, 107, 108, 118, 119, 131, 132,
    137, 140

F

Fant, J. C. 61, 69
Farley, Robert 61, 74, 97, 98, 101
Finkelstein, Martin 151, 153
Finley, Robert H. 10
Fleming, Horace 23, 141-143, 147, 152
Foerster, Alma Pauline 17, 21, 30, 31, 74
Fogelsong, Robert H. 146, 147
Foote, Henry Stuart 16
Ford, Jennifer 8
Fortune, Porter L. 8, 150
Foster, Jack D. 135, 140
Foster Study 135
Frazer, Robert 42, 48
Fulton, Robert 46, 51, 52
funding formula 123, 135-137

G

Gainey, John Lee 83
George, James Z. 43, 44, 48, 85, 101
George, Jennings B. 79, 83, 93
Gibbs, Phillip L. 121
Gibson, Joseph E. 93, 94, 101, 131
Gibson Study 94, 101
Giles, William 119, 120, 125150
Gill, Craig 8
Goodman, William 138
Graham, Hardy Poindexter 60, 66, 70, 72,
    74-76, 88
Green, James Earl 121
Green, Wigfall 73, 74, 76
Guice, John D. W. 17

H

Haile, William 12
Hampstead Academy 13
Hardy, John C. 50
Harkey, Ira 106, 113
Harper, Frank 85
Harrison, Bobby 144, 150, 152, 153
Harrison, Lisa 8
Harrison, Robert 132
Harry Truman's Commission on Higher
    Education 92
Harvard College 7, 9, 17, 33, 35, 40, 41,
    131
Hederman, Tom 107
Helfrich, Bob 99

Hemingway, William 62
Henry, Aaron 119
Henry, J. M. 26
Herrin, Bob 107
Higate, W. B. 45
Hightower, George R. 54
Hilgard, Eugene 28, 35, 47
Hilliard, Elbert 8
Hiram Revels 37
Historically Black Colleges and Universities 138
    HBCU 139, 145, 149, 152
Holmes Collection 8, 101, 113, 114, 125, 139, 140
Holmes, George Frederick 25
Holmes, Verner 8, 59, 105, 106, 113, 114, 116, 119, 120, 123-126, 129, 130 139
House Bill 242 83-86
Hudson, John 72, 73, 75
Hudson, Roy 8, 147
Hume, Alfred 57, 60-62, 64-68, 70, 74, 79, 81, 82, 88
Humphrey, George Duke 80, 82, 93
Hutchins, Robert Maynard 7

I

Industrial Institute and College 39, 41, 42, 48, 52, 54-56
Ivey, Susan 8

J

Jackson State riot 120, 122, 126
Jackson State University 43, 86, 88, 100, 101, 118, 120-122, 126, 129-133, 138, 145
J. D. Williams Library 8
Jefferson College 10-13, 15, 18, 19, 24, 30, 139
Jefferson, Thomas 9, 10
Johnson, Greg 8
Johnson, Joseph E. 135, 140
Johnson, Paul 60, 82, 83, 85-87, 109, 110, 115
Johnson report 135
Jones County Junior College 116
Jones, Dan 149, 150, 152
Jones, Richard W. 42, 45, 48
Jordan, David 147

K

Keady, William 119, 125
Keirn, Nellie 69
Kennard, Clyde 98, 99, 101
Kennedy, John 105, 110-115
Kennedy, Robert 105, 108, 110-115, 118
Kent State 121, 126
Kethley, William 69
Khayat, Robert 150
Kincannon, Andrew 42, 48, 54
King, Clennon 98, 103

L

LaBauve Fund 78
Lamar, L. Q. C. 27, 30, 44
Latham, Joe 107
Layzell, Tom 142
Lee, Stephen D. 39, 40, 48, 49
Leming, Jessica 8
Lesher, Steven 121, 122, 126
Limbert, Claudia 145, 146, 152
Lomax, W. A. 65
Longino, Andrew H. 49, 59
Longstreet, Augustus Baldwin 15, 19, 25-31
low pressure faction 63
Loyola University 116
Lucas, Aubrey 143, 150
Lucas, Christopher J. 151, 153

M

Marshall, Burke 109, 112
Marston, Robert 124, 126
Mayes, Edward 19, 31, 44, 46, 48
May, Joseph 85, 88
Mayo, Brad 150
McAllister, James 12
McCain, William D. 14, 19, 74, 75, 91, 100, 101
McCarthy, James "Babe" 116
McCaughan, John J. 24
McGee, Meredith Coleman 113
McGuinness, Aims C. 127, 139, 153
McNutt, Alexander G. 16, 17, 19
McRae, John J. 26, 27-29
McShane, James 108-110
McWhite, Leigh 8
Memphis State 116, 117

Meredith, James 100, 103-115
Meredith, Tom 147
Millsaps 43
Minor, Bill 105
mission statement 97, 133, 140
Mississippi Agricultural and Mechanical College 39-41, 43, 44, 49, 53-55, 70
    Mississippi A&M 39-41, 43-46, 48-50, 52, 54-56, 61, 64, 68-72, 75
    see also Mississippi State University
Mississippi City 22
Mississippi College 18, 24, 43
Mississippi Normal School 52
Mississippi State College 79, 81, 92, 99
Mississippi State College for Women 56, 70, 81, 93, 95, 96
    MSCW 57, 61, 68-72, 77, 79, 83, 93-95
    see also Mississippi University for Women
Mississippi State Teachers College 57
Mississippi State University 44, 48, 77, 95
    see also Mississippi Agricultural and Mechanical College
Mississippi University for Women, 39, 48
    see also Mississippi State College for Women
Mississippi Valley State University 101, 135, 147, 149, 152
Mississippi Vocational College 94, 97
Mitchell, Dennis 8, 17
Mitchell, Fred Tom 95
Mitchell, Jerry 99, 152
Mize, Sidney 104
Montgomery, G. V. 122
Moore, Carroll Chiles 8
Morgan, Chester 8, 72, 74, 75, 76, 148, 152
Morrill Land Grant Act 37
Morris, Willie 112, 114
Motley, Constance Baker 104
Mounger, William 107, 110, 114
Murphree, Dennis 61

N

NAACP Legal Defense Fund 103
Newman, Lester 149

Nixon, Richard 121
Noel, Edmund F. 53
North, Linton Glover 64
Norwood, W. D. 118

O

Oakland College 16, 19, 37
Old Time College 14–16, 25, 29, 35, 41, 130, 151
Ole Miss 8, 30, 44, 51, 52, 54, 55, 57, 59, 61, 62, 64-68, 70-73, 77, 80, 84, 92, 94, 96-98, 100, 101, 103-106, 111-114, 116-119, 123, 125, 130-132, 134, 142, 145, 147, 149, 150,
Oliver, Donna H. 149, 152
organized anarchies 7, 151, 153
O'Shea, Michael V. 58-60, 62, 66, 78, 80, 94
Oxford 22, 23, 26, 29, 34, 38, 39, 54, 58, 62, 64, 65, 74, 94, 98, 101, 109-111, 113, 117, 118, 139, 140, 150

P

Parchman 99
Pawley, Tara 8
Peabody Study 80-82, 88
pecking order 95, 96, 123
Peoples, John 120, 121, 129
Percy, William Alexander 73, 76
Phillips, Rubel 115
Pieschel, Bridget Smith 47, 48, 60, 75, 88, 101
Piliawsky, Monte 118, 125
Pipes, William H. 93, 101
Powell, Robert 52
Powers, Joseph Neely 57, 61, 70, 71, 73, 79
President's Commission on Campus Unrest 120, 121, 126

Q

Quitman, John Anthony 16

R

Rainey, Kenneth 118
Raspberry, William 138
Reddix, Jacob 93
rednecks 46, 48, 59

Reneau, Sallie Eola 38, 39, 47, 48
Rent, Clyda 69, 142, 152
Revels, Hiram 37, 38, 47
Revolution of 1875 38
Rholes, Julia 8
Rice, James 86
Roberts, Johnny 98, 99
Roberts, M. M. 115-120, 123-126
Rogers, Lauren 8
Rudolph, Frederick 7, 13, 14, 17-19, 30, 33, 47, 89
Russell, Lee 55, 56
Rust College, 36, 47

S

Salisbury, Leila 8
Sanger, W. T. 93, 94
Saunders, Martha Dunagin 148, 149, 152
Scarborough, William 148
Schauber, Ambrose B. 56, 70
Schuster, Jack 151, 153
seminary fund 11, 21, 23, 24, 43
Semple Broaddus College 14
Senate Concurrent Resolution 522 144
    SCR 522 144, 145
Sexton, James 52, 60
Shaffer, Molly Beth 8
Shands, Garvin 51, 52
Sharkey, William L. 34
Shattuck 15
Shattuck, David O. 15
Sheldon, George L. 55
Sheldon-Zeller bill 55, 61
Silver, James W. 113, 117, 118, 125
Simrall, Horatio Fleming 23
Smith, Theodore 84, 131
Smith, William H. 83
Southern Association of Colleges and Schools 65, 73, 89
State Board of Education 36, 58
State Normal School 36, 38, 41, 45, 50
State Sovereignty Commission 98-101
State Teachers College 57, 61, 66, 69, 77, 79, 81-83, 85, 93
Stennis, John C. 86, 89
Stetar, Joseph 33, 34, 47
Stevens, Boswell 129
Stewart, Alexander P. 35
Stone, John M. 36, 38, 39, 47, 114

Strickler, George 118
Strobel, James 137
Sullens, Fred 54, 63, 68, 72, 73, 83, 86
Summer, A. F. 122
Sutherland, Robert E. Lee 66-69, 79
Sydnor, Charles 18, 30, 71

T

Taylor, Joseph W. 34, 47
Thames, Shelby 147, 148, 152
The Greater University of Mississippi 64, 68, 74, 77
Thelin, John 141, 146, 152
The New Republic 72, 75
Thomas, Matt 145, 152
Thompson, Jacob 26
Thompson, W. O. 73
Thrash, E. E. 119, 132, 137, 140
Tollison, Gray 150, 153
Tougaloo University 36
Triplett, Edward H. 46
Trister, Michael 118
Tubb, Thomas 107, 108, 114
Turner, R. Gerald 136, 140, 150
Turner, Thomas 62, 74128, 129

U

Universitas Scientiarum 29, 31
University of Mississippi 22-32, 34, 37, 41, 43, 45, 53, 54, 56, 58, 59, 60, 94, 103, 118, 149
unwritten law 14, 116

V

Vardaman, James K. 46, 50-52, 59

W

Waddel, John Newton 24, 28, 31, 34, 35, 37, 38, 47, 92
Waites, Hilton 84
Walker, Buz M.
    Jr. 56, 68-70
    Sr. 56
Waller, William 124, 127-129, 139
Walton, Thomas L. 34, 35
Washington, Walter 99, 150
Watkins, Tom 109, 110, 112

Watson, Vance 147
West, Phillip 141
Whitehorn, Stanley 8
White, Hugh Lawson 82-85, 111
White, John 150
White, Neil 8
Whitfield, Henry L. 55-58, 60-62, 98
Wilkerson, E. C. 24
Williams, J. D. 91, 92, 96, 98-101, 103,
    106, 112, 113, 117, 119, 150
Williams, John Bell 121, 122
Williams, John Sharp 51
Wisconsin Idea 58
Wisdom, John Minor 104
Wood, Sanford 118
Woolfolk building 108
Wright, Fielding 91
Wyatt, Kent 150

Y

Yarbrough, Roosevelt 149

Z

Zacharias, Donald 136, 150
Zeller, Julius C. 55, 64, 71, 75

www.ingramcontent.com/pod-product-compliance
Lightning Source LLC
LaVergne TN
LVHW041336080426
835512LV00006B/481